A CHRISTIAN-COMMUNIST DIALOGUE

A Christian-Communist Dialogue

Roger Garaudy and Quentin Lauer, S.J.

1968

Doubleday & Company, Inc., Garden City, New York

Library of Congress Catalog Card Number 68–27118
Copyright © 1968 by Quentin Lauer and Doubleday & Company, Inc.
All Rights Reserved
Printed in the United States of America
First Edition

CONTENTS

CONTENTS

INTRODUCTION

A number of recent events, not the least of which was the interested and enthusiastic response of the reading public to a book by one of the present authors, *From Anathema to Dialogue*,[1] has led us to the inescapable conclusion that a serious Marxist-Christian dialogue is not only a contemporary desideratum but also a very concrete possibility. Already this dialogue has been carried on in a variety of ways and in a variety of circumstances —and its results have been encouraging. For the most part, however, the participants in the dialogue have been theoreticians who, while they have already delineated the intellectual bases for fruitful discussion between the opposed parties, have not made conflicting views come to grips with each other in the concrete manner which the present state of Marxist-Christian relations demands. It may be, perhaps, that the only level upon which dialogue is as yet feasible is a highly intellectual one. It seems, nevertheless, imperative that the arena in which the discussion takes place must be the open forum accessible to all, the uninformed as well as the informed, the non-professional as well as the professional, the man in the street as well as the expert.

In the present book we shall attempt to engage in just

such a concrete dialogue, in which we hope the reading audience will engage with as much enthusiasm and mutual respect as we do. If concrete dialogue, however, is to be more than a pious wish, it seems necessary first of all to clear the ground for action by establishing some of the conditions for fruitful dialogue and by ruling out the sorts of attitudes according to which each of the opposing parties either seeks to prevail over the other at all costs or, what is equally sterile, both sides direct all their energies to futile mutual admiration. Since in the present instance it is simply impossible to ignore the political overtones inseparable from dialogue, each of us must resist the temptation to make political capital of the mere fact of dialogue—the only legitimate advantage to be sought is that of mutual enlightenment.

At the outset, then, there are disguised forms of non-dialogue to be avoided. The first of these is what we might call the "dialogue of the deaf," where each party is concerned only with talking, not with listening, only with uncovering what is worst in the words and deeds of the other. It is called dialogue, but at best it is preparing oneself for a crusade or a fight to the death. Implied in this, of course, is the simplistic view that existence is one gigantic struggle of good against evil—and that to dialogue is to take up arms for the good. A more humane but no less ineffective form of nondialogue is that of the disincarnated minds, whose discussion takes place—very successfully—on such an elevated plane of abstraction that it has no relation to or effect upon the real world where life is lived. The positions which are discussed are real enough, and the effect they have on human beings is real too, but the aspect under which they are discussed is ideal. Although there is no denying that such an exchange can be useful, especially since it tends to involve an honest presentation of positive views, it still fails to touch men's lives where they are most real.

The most subtle form of nondialogue in the sophisticated world is what we can call the "dialogue of self-accusation," where each of the interlocutors examines his historical conscience in public. The Christian, for example, recognizes that the Christian God has been for too long one who fills the gaps in scientific knowledge, thus inhibiting the advance of science and not permitting the Christian to recognize science's autonomy. By the same token the Christian confesses that his philosophy has been ineffective by its dualistic otherworldliness (what Nietzsche called "a poor man's Platonism"). It opposes God and the world and then tells man that to find God he must abandon the world. Coming even closer to the heart of Christian living the Christian may strike his breast and admit that Christianity has been so dedicated to personal piety—or, worse still, to personal salvation—that it has neglected man's responsibility to change the world. This sort of Christianity finds so much significance in the past, e.g. seeing the sacraments as renewals, that it fails to understand concrete man whose hope is in the future. Part and parcel of this latter aberration is Christianity's historical identification with the status quo ever since the time of Constantine—social evil is dismissed as God's will, even in much of the "social doctrine" of the Church.

In this form of nondialogue the Marxist will not be outdone; he too must turn the critical searchlight on the faults of his own side. He can see a corruption of dialectic materialism in a tendency to revert to mechanistic forms of eighteenth-century French materialism. More than that, he can recognize that Marxists have been naïve about history, seeing in it an instance of the "dialectic of nature," thus "scientizing" it beyond all credence. If he is a very sophisticated Marxist he recognizes in "socialist realism" a large dose of idealism, of utopianism and messianism. By the same token he recognizes that unsophisticated

Marxists have tended to identify humanity with the proletariat and the proletariat with the party. Out of this, he knows, has come Stalin's sacralization of the party and the tendency to confuse criticism with apostasy.

When Christians and Marxists have finished making these admissions about themselves, it turns out that they have not been speaking to each other at all. They may in a subtle way have contributed to their own smug satisfaction at being so "honest," but more than likely they have succeeded only in covering up their own real weaknesses. This does not mean, however, that there is no place in dialogue for honest self-criticism on both sides, criticism of both principle and practice. Out of just such criticism can come an honest evaluation of the possible contributions which both can make to the results that both want as well as an effort to estimate the possibilities of development or modification in both positions. If, however, neither side gets beyond this soul-baring self-accusation (with its tendency to be hysterical), dialogue has not been advanced at all—there is no genuine confrontation. Granted that neither side can shut its eyes to the past and that, therefore, both criticism and self-criticism in this area can be valid, it can be justified only if it is historical, looking to the past only to the extent that it is still significant for the present and then turns to the future, seeking practical consequences in the realm of effective cooperation toward the building of a better world.

This sort of concrete effectiveness can be achieved only if dialogue is carried on without skepticism. Difference of opinion cannot be accompanied by denial of truth or by despair of attaining it; it simply points to the need of relinquishing the dogmatic in favor of the dialectical approach to truth. At the same time the dialectical approach must be without illusions. We who here enter into dialogue cannot claim that our opinions necessarily represent those of our respective communities, and still we cannot forget that we remain throughout responsible to those same communities. This is delicate: Knowing that at any point one or the other can be repudiated by his community, still we can go on only if we are sustained by the hope that in doing so we are engaging more than ourselves as individuals. In this connection it is obviously difficult to foresee what the reading public will expect from this sort of exchange. If reactions already received are any indication, some will be interested to discover which side "wins," they will see the whole enterprise as a debate, in which the force of logic—or rhetoric—will demand concessions from one side or the other. The side which makes the fewest concessions will walk off with the victory. Others may very well look for vigorous position-statements from both sides, which will clearly delineate the over-all opposition between them. We ourselves, acutely conscious that neither of us knows the other side adequately, hopefully look for a clear understanding of the degree to which we can and cannot agree and—perhaps more significantly—a clearer and more honest understanding, each of his own position, brought about by a confrontation guided on both sides by a sincere concern for the future of man on this earth.

This honest confrontation is rendered particularly imperative by the fact that, as we move into the last third of the twentieth century, the world is undergoing a metamorphosis unprecedented in its history. It is a world whose unification has been made possible by rapidly developing means of human communication, on the level of thought and on that of practical action, and still it remains a pluralist world.

The pluralism in question, however, is not necessarily one in which men are separated in skepticism and despair. It is based, rather, on a new, operational conception of cognition and by the advance of peoples to the stage of maturity and adulthood. The developments manifested

in the sciences of man, the affirmation, outside the traditional occident, of new centers of historical initiative
with their creation of values, the factual diversity among
human models of the social order in an age of new scientific and technical revolution—all of these "signs of our
times" demand new vigilance on the part of men, for hos-
tile confrontations under our present technical conditions
would lead to the suicide of nations and, perhaps, of
our planet. By the same token, they demand a new creative effort, for new and unheard-of perspectives are opening up to peoples for the construction of their future.

The need for spiritual renovation has reached the stage
of consciousness of self both in all great conceptions of the
world and in all the great human communities, face to
face with the demands of modern times.

Now, it is just this sort of coming-to-consciousness
which has impelled the Church of the Council, with
Popes John XXIII and Paul VI, to institute a dialogue
with the world and, in order to make it as fruitful as
possible, to distinguish more profoundly in the Church's
own message that which is fundamental from that which
has simply been tied to the institutional or cultural forms
in which this message has historically been expressed.
This double movement, which John XXIII called
"aggiornamento," has not ceased to reveal its vivifying
power. It is developing along the same lines and with
the same efficacy in the other Christian churches.[2]

From a radically different viewpoint, in the course of
the last ten years the Communists have felt that it is a
necessity both of their own teaching and of our common
history to make themselves open to others, expecting
from them a development and an enrichment of the
truths they feel are theirs to give. Communists have recognized the necessity of a dialogue which would at one
and the same time be their own self-affirmation and an

integration of the intellectual and human contribution which other spiritual families have to give.

These are but two examples among others of a universal aspiration which is being affirmed with increasing force within Protestantism as well as in the Jewish consciousness, at the heart of Islam as well as among the peoples of Asia, Africa, and Latin America.

Philosophical differences may well be irreducible. Moral agreements seem to all to be possible, real, necessary for the construction of men's common future. In a great new human encounter such as this, dialogues have already been instituted. Various publications have chosen as a sort of banner the beautiful title "dialogue," thus contributing to a more profound understanding and a mutual enrichment.

As we envisage the dialogue, then, it can and should take place on three levels. (1) There is a first level of necessary agreement and cooperation, which means not only mutual respect for each other's sincerity but also agreement regarding concrete ends to be attained. We must agree in seeking to abolish the very possibility of atomic war, to alleviate the wretched conditions under which the vast majority of men live, to render impossible the exploitation of some men by others. At this level our respective attitudes to the world can be illuminated without demanding that positions required by our common history be identified with any fixed concept of the world. (2) There is, then, a second level of what we might call converging moralities. The future of the world is to be our common future, and in seeking to formulate this common future it is perfectly legitimate for us to ask each other, "What is it that you wish to make of man?" Here we can start with real philosophical differences (e.g. in our concept of man) and still end up united in defense of values which we hold in common. Although we may not mean exactly the same thing when we speak of these values, we can agree in the following statement of purpose: to make of each and every man a true man, that is, a center of initiative, responsibility, and creativeness. Here it is not inconceivable that we might be led to ask ourselves, What sort of possibility is there that a Christian should be a Communist, or a Communist a Christian? There can be no dialogue where either of the parties refuses to admit that his own position can be radically changed as a result of discussion. (3) The third level is one on which the differences are not only real but irreducible; it is the level of contradiction between atheist materialism and Christian faith. On this level there is no exclusion of either dialogue or cooperation on the first two levels, nor need there be an absence of a third kind of dialogue, where agreement consists in a sympathetic understanding of disagreement, recognizing that not only disagreement but also agreement may be more superficial than they seem. We might say that precisely on this level dialogue becomes most imperative, indispensable for both the Christian and the Communist. The basic divergence of position regards the meaning of human autonomy, and in this regard each position constitutes for the other a significant counterbalance. Atheism plays a purifying role for the Christian by preventing him from adoring a false, man-degrading god; and Christian faith for its part awakens the atheistic humanist to the necessity of remaining open to transcendence—if not of God, at least of man. It would be worse than naïve to see the divergence here as an opposition between humanism and theism—both sides can and should be eminently humanistic—but it does highlight the problem of two opposed humanisms: Which of the two more concretely gives to man the responsibility for his own history and the effective means for building his own future?

Since the third level of dialogue is that on which the two positions are genuinely contradictory, a word should be said on contradictions. There would seem to be three basic attitudes which can be taken in relation to contradiction—apart from the falsely irenic one of not recognizing it as a contradiction. (1) The contradiction is simply allowed to remain; no attempt is made to resolve it, and mutually contradictory positions are left unreconciled. With this, dialogue comes to an end. (2) Since of two contradictory positions only one can be true, each regards his own position as the only valid one, seeing no possibility that the other may be partially right or his own partially wrong. The only effort that each makes is to silence the other. Here dialogue does not even begin. (3) Contradiction is recognized as possibly fruitful if opposing positions are allowed to confront each other, modify each other, and possibly be reconciled in a third position which does justice to both. Here there is genuine dialogue, the only kind in which honest human beings can justifiably engage. It demands, however, unremitting effort and a constant refusal to despair.

Where the concrete dialogue in question is that between Christian and Communist, there are a number of built-in obstacles which have to be obviated if the dialogue is to get off the ground at all. Some of the attitudes which constitute just such obstacles are the following:

1) A kind of belief in God (or a belief in the kind of God) which actually does constitute an alienation of man's true humanity. Philosophers from Plato to Marx or Nietzsche have inveighed against this kind of God.
2) The kind of utopian idealism which uncritically sees the solution to all human ills in a "classless society," which is conceivable only as the negation of known forms of society but whose positive inadequacies have yet to reveal themselves.
3) An authentic religious conviction which is marred by

an irrational suspicion that all refusal to share it involves
more or less serious moral fault.

4) An enthusiasm for the historical dialectic which is
misled by Marx's own characterization of it as "scientific"
into thinking that it shares the exactitude of contemporary
natural science.

5) An emphasis on the supernatural to the point of being
blind to or downgrading the natural—the real "opium
of the people."

6) A conviction that the refusal of a supernatural explanation is equivalent to finding a natural one. This last is
in effect the same as the previous one, since it arbitrarily
sets up an irreducible opposition between natural and
supernatural.

There is one other difficulty which arises only partially
from the fact that one of us is a Communist and the other
a Christian; it arises also from the fact that one of us is
an American and the other a Frenchman. It is the difficulty of language—but not in the obvious sense that one
of us speaks French and the other English. Rather it
is that, to use language at all is to run the risk of ambiguity. Thus, when one of us affirms and the other denies,
we may well be using the same words, but what we are
affirming and denying may not be the same. Some words
may have overtones—emotive, evaluative, significative—
for a Frenchman which they do not for an American, and
vice versa. There will be times when we do not *mean*
the same thing by the words we use; there may even be
times when we do not "mean" the same thing by "meaning." The difficulty is not insuperable, but we cannot hope
that the final result will be the complete absence of
ambiguities.

Our aim in all that has been said up to this point has
been to outline the conditions for a dialogue, whose

necessity would seem to be obvious if society (or civilization) is to survive. To speak of society or of civilization, however, is to speak of man—of all men. If the Christian-Communist dialogue in which we engage is to be significant and effective it must stand for all the major confrontations which today's world—and the future of man—demand. In a sense it does this by bringing face to face the two most basically opposed concepts of man, the theistic and the atheistic. The dialogue, however, will be fruitless if it does not involve those other great witnesses to the opposition between man and man: capital vs. labor, East vs. West, the developed and underdeveloped peoples of the globe. We cannot limit ourselves to a dialogue between occidentals or even to an East-West dialogue; ultimately only a dialogue which involves all civilizations can be viable. Civilizations must learn to coexist, if they are to exist at all—but this means working together in a common effort toward achieving the brotherhood of man. It is our hope that the sort of dialogue in which we here engage will contribute to the eventual realization of this brotherhood.

I THE STATE OF THE DIALOGUE

Lauer:

One of the most perplexing questions in a dialogue such as the one in which we have committed ourselves to engage is the question of where and how to begin. It is true, of course, that we are by no means initiators of the over-all dialogue between Marxists and Christians, but there is a very real sense in which we are beginning something new by reducing to print what can only with great difficulty retain the spontaneity of the spoken give-and-take. By way of facilitating the entry, then, I shall take the liberty of addressing myself to opinions which you have already published—chiefly in *From Anathema to Dialogue* and *Marxisme du XX*ᵉ *siècle*[1]—regarding not only the dialogue itself but also the relation between Marxism and religion in general. Before beginning, however, it might be well to clear the ground in such a way as to insure that what ensues is indeed dialogue and not merely an exchange of opinions or, worse still, a double monologue. We must speak to each other, and we must do so in a manner which will insure that the exchange is fruitful for both of us—and, above all, for the humanity we both hope to represent.

We are both without question heirs to a mutual hatred and mistrust which on both sides has produced much mischief for which we can and should both be sorry. Neither of us should, I think, feel compelled to attack or defend this mischief in order to safeguard the purity of his own position—mutual recriminations are not likely to advance the end we have in view. By the same token, the whole question of dialogue tends to be accompanied by a fear on both sides (sometimes justified) that the other side seeks dialogue only when it can see in it an instrument of political advantage. From the beginning, then, each of us should resist the temptation to see in dialogue a means of promoting a political position. Strictly speaking, the questions which confront us are not those of conflicting political positions—even though, historically speaking, Christian-Communist opposition has more often than not had political overtones. The fact remains that, to carry on the discussion at the level of politics is to falsify the dialogue; for, whatever may be the Marxist's commitments at this level, the Christian, simply as Christian, is not committed to the support of any political position—unless, of course, we say in the abstract that he should be committed to that position which he is convinced best safeguards and promotes the dignity of man as such. This in turn means that, if the Christian *de facto* opposes Communism, his reason for so doing must be a conviction that it does not safeguard and promote this dignity—although, apart from his Christianity, he may on other grounds be opposed to it politically. The point is that there is no more reason for the Christian to accuse Communism as such of its aberrations, e.g. Stalinism or Mao's Red Guard, than there is for the Communist to charge Christianity as such with the horrors of the Crusades or the Inquisition, although I should like to be assured that you repudiate Communist aberrations as vigorously as I do those to which Christian history is a witness.

It might not be amiss at this point for both of us to say something of the concrete dialogue, to which we referred in our Introduction, from the standpoint of the experience which each of us has had.

If I were to speak here of Christian-Marxist dialogue in the United States I should, I am afraid, have little to say. We have, it is true, watched with considerable interest and even enthusiasm developments in other parts of the world—not only the beginnings of theoretical discussion but also practical efforts to overcome existing tensions between the representatives of two opposing world views—but only sporadically do we engage in concrete efforts at mutual understanding. The reasons for this are varied, but chief among them, I suspect, is the fact that Marxist influence within the United States is so negligible that even those who worry about it on the world scene treat it as something of a domestic curiosity. Only recently have Americans—and only a few of them—begun to realize that Marxist theory is intellectually respectable and that Marxist practice may well have to be re-evaluated. Christians, for example, are finding more and more often that, in their struggles against war or for civil rights, those who are genuinely concerned to struggle along with them may well be Communists (or at least Marxists). We are prompted to take a new look at developments in Cuba and South America, in Poland or Yugoslavia, and what we find is the possibility that beneath the clash of political aims may be hidden a similarity of humanitarian aspirations.

Corresponding to Christian interest in Communism, however, we find little evidence of more than the mildest Communist interest in Christianity. I cannot, of course, speak for the whole country, but my own experience of dialogue is that when it occurs at all it occurs under Christian auspices. It is not without significance, I think, that in the three international meetings to promote Christian-Communist dialogue sponsored by the *Paulusgesellschaft*, American Communists have been conspicuous by their absence (as, incidentally, have been Soviet Communists). It may, of course, be that American Communists are faced with problems which participation in international dialogue will do little to solve. In that case we can only hope that the need for dialogue on the domestic scene will be recognized and met. Perhaps we can hope that one of the results of what you and I are doing here will be precisely that.

In any event, what we are doing, I think, is responding to a call to which no one should remain deaf. In doing so we are recognizing a certain basic identity of ideal, even where our conceptions of the means of attaining that ideal are different and sometimes even antagonistic. More than that, we are recognizing that neither Communism nor Christianity will attain this ideal by trying to go it alone.

The call to dialogue, then, is precisely the call sent out to each of us not to try to go it alone. If it can be assumed that both of us desire not only the survival of the human race but also its constant progress in becoming more authentically human, it can also be assumed that we see dialogue as an inescapable necessity, without which the aim will not be accomplished. At the same time, however, we must recognize the partial character of what we are doing, contributing in but a small way to the ongoing dialogue which in the future must characterize the relationship between all attempts to achieve this end within a framework of supernatural belief and attempts to do so through a negation of precisely this belief. There is no way of reconciling a concept of man which sees him as incompletely man if he does not believe with one which sees him as incompletely man if he does believe. But this does not mean that we need be incapable of seeing that neither conception of man can afford not to listen to the other—remembering, of course, that in listening to one or the other one is not listening to a single voice.

Garaudy:

In France—as in Italy and Spain—the dialogue between Christians and Marxists has a prehistory. It belongs to the time when, for Christians, Socialism and Communism were the earthly incarnation of evil, the work of the devil, and when the revolutionaries identified Christianity with the forces of oppression, of exploitation, and of counter-revolution, giving to these forces "the spiritual aroma" of its metaphysical justifications.

It has been historical evolution itself which has enabled the dialogue to become a historical reality. A danger which is both enduring and universal in scope has served to bring Marxist and Christian close to each other for a common defense of man. Now that it is technically possible, with atomic and thermonuclear bombs, to put an end to the human story which began two million years ago, thus wiping out whatever meaning the life and history of men on earth might have had, it has become more and more evident that it would be impossible to construct man's future without believers (still less in opposition to them) or without the Communists (still less in opposition to them).

This new worldwide situation has made even more evident the historical necessity of the "outstretched hand" policy, inaugurated by French Communists in 1935. The first great response to this was the encyclical *Pacem in Terris* of Pope John XXIII.

From that point forward the dialogue has broadened

in scope. In its history it is possible to distinguish three essential phases.

The first, which lasted approximately ten years and which entered a new phase only in 1967, was a preparatory period of discussing the *possibility of dialogue*. It was characterized by a tendency to situate problems solely on the level of theory. Still, it was an indispensable stage—that of learning to distinguish various levels of confrontation, to avoid confusing three levels: the political, the moral, and that of a conception of the world.

a) On the level of politics it was possible to establish a *de facto*, practical cooperation, concerned with immediate problems: the struggle against colonialist wars and political oppression and for the amelioration of living conditions, etc. This was accompanied by the possibility of reciprocal criticism concerning the historical solidarity of the churches with the forces of social conservatism or the dogmatic and stultifying deformations of Marxism.

b) On the level of morality it was possible to define common, properly human values, which we had to defend and which involved defining our moral agreements.

c) It was on the level of our conceptions of the world that irreducible disagreements appeared, which, however, permitted each side to become more profoundly aware of what was fundamental in his own position and of what was simply tied to the cultural or institutional forms which could characterize either Christianity or Marxism at different periods of their histories.

The most positive result of all this was that each side understood that it had something to learn from the other. Marxists learned that, if, in the cultural heritage of the past, they underestimated the Christian moment, their humanism risked being a closed humanism (e.g. resembling that of the eighteenth-century French materialists), contrary to the very spirit of Marxism. As for Christians, more and more of them realize that, if they are unable to integrate the lessons of Marxism regarding the role of structures and determinisms in crushing or liberating man and regarding the methods of action calculated to dominate these structures and determinisms, their Christianity is in great danger of evaporating into a purely personal piety which forgets the Christian's social responsibilities toward the construction of man's future.

This first period, then, has been fruitful, and in this direction an extraordinary effort toward clarification should be undertaken. This is true, because not all confusions have been eliminated, nor is it evident either to all Christians or to all Communists that this dialogue and cooperation is necessary, not only tactically (with a view to an efficacious construction of a common future), but also from the point of view of principle (in order to enrich our respective conceptions).

There could, however, be no question of waiting until this penetration should be complete, until all forms of conservatism and sectarianism are overcome, before passing on to a new stage.

We cannot ask indefinitely what are the conditions for the possibility of dialogue: There is already proof that it is possible and necessary; the theory of dialogue has already been outlined. What is more, the urgency not only of a philosophical dialogue but also of practical cooperation manifests itself more and more.

The most fortunate effect which this first form of dialogue can have produced is to have brought about a situation where its objectives have been attained in such a way as to have been outdistanced by history, with the result that new tasks have arisen.

This outdistancing is taking place. This is true, first of all, because parallel to theoretical discussions there have developed forms of practical cooperation: In France, for example, one could mention unified action involving Christian unions and unions of the C.G.T., common cause against the colonialist war in Algeria, cooperation in the struggle for disarmament and for the prohibition of atomic arms, the campaign against American intervention in Vietnam.

This practical cooperation has never been subordinated to the conclusions of theoretical dialogues, nor has common intellectual investigation ever demanded as a condition the adoption of a political position. Still, the two parallel, independent efforts have been mutually nourished, fecundated, and reinforced: Once theoretical prejudices and confusions have been overcome, obstacles to a common effort have been overcome at the same time, and action has been strengthened. By the same token the human solidarity born of common action has facilitated the exchange of ideas and has stimulated the desire for a more profound understanding of motives on each side and for a critical assimilation of the portion of truth which each contained and from which each drew its strength to fight.

What characterizes the second phase of the dialogue is, first of all, a growing interdependence of the two forms manifested by the approach to the problem of Marxist-Christian relationships. This is a demand for *action*, for once we go beyond immediate problems to the long-term question of a nation's future, or of man's, it is no longer possible to put in parentheses the conception of the world and of man which inspires the action of each. To refuse this basic dialogue would be to limit common action to a succession of *defensive* operations against immediate dangers.

This is a demand of theoretical dialogue also: If it were not to result in a cooperative action to change the world and to make it more human, such a dialogue would become dry and academic, an end in itself, a parlor game for beautiful souls. It would be not only sterile but also harmful: It would be a distraction and would serve as an alibi for avoiding concrete historical tasks.

It is remarkable that it should be in Spain, in the common struggle against Francoist fascism, that dialogue and cooperation should have reached their highest levels, both in action—in strikes, street demonstrations, in legal and illegal political organization—and theoretically, where great theologians have brought to the problems a profound theology of profane values and of revolution, and where the Spanish Communist party, freed from sectarianism, has made an important original contribution to the *total Marxist reflection on religious problems* and on theoretical and practical relations with Christians.

The second phase began when Christians and Communists, no longer limiting themselves to a common reflection on the conditions for the possibility of dialogue, held a meeting, international in scope, at Geneva in October 1967, to study in common concrete problems. On the initiative of the World Council of Churches, Protestants, Orthodox Christians, Roman Catholics, and Marxists, chose as a first theme of theoretical investigations—before entering upon a program of practical cooperation—the consequences for human development of technical and economic progress in the already highly industrialized countries as well as in developing countries.

Moving to this second stage implied no longer being satisfied with merely sporadic publication of writings in which theologians and Marxist philosophers confronted each other. It demanded the creation of a permanent organ of dialogue for a larger audience. Beginning in September 1968, there will be published a review edited by two Christians—Father Chenu, O.P., and Pastor Cazalis, professor on the Protestant theology faculty at Paris—and by two Communists—Roger Garaudy, a Frenchman, and Manuel Azcorate, a Spaniard. Its policy is that all are most free to express their criticisms and that all have the right to reply, but that no article may be published without *unanimous* agreement of the board.

Thus a new impulse has been given to both theoretical dialogue and practical cooperation. Still, at a time when the countries of Europe and North America can no longer pretend to be sole centers of historical initiative and sole creators of values, this dialogue would, in its turn, be quickly superseded by history and would take on a "provincial" character did it not quickly become a "dialogue of civilizations," with Asia, Africa, and Latin America.

That will be the third great stage in the dialogue—which should be begun at almost the same time as the second, for a too-great gap would throw doubt on the very principle of the dialogue which is at once a recognition of *pluralism* and a mutual fertilization through an openness to all creative contributions and to a continuous creation of man, of his world, and of history.

II CHRISTIANITY AND ATHEISM

Lauer:

Now that we have ironed out—to a certain extent—
the difficulties of dialogue and after we have reached
some sort of agreement as to what dialogue is to be
about, it would seem time that we actually speak to each
other. Abrupt as it may seem, then, the way to begin,
I take it, is to speak of difficulties which are inseparable
from our being on different sides of a fence. How fundamental these difficulties are remains to be seen, but in any
event they cannot be shrugged aside.

At the outset I should like to make it clear that, whatever difficulties I may experience with regard to Communism, they are not primarily political. As a Christian I
am committed to the support of that which I am convinced best safeguards and promotes the dignity of man.
In many instances this commitment can, of course,
place me in opposition to what might be called official
positions in my own Church or, at least, with positions
represented by important segments of that Church's
hierarchy. The point is, however, that it can also place me

in opposition to Communism as I understand it. The difficulties I experience in my approach to Communism—or to Marxism, if you prefer—spring from a serious concern as to whether it does, in fact, safeguard and promote the dignity of man. Nor do I refer here to such phenomena as Stalinism, Mao's Red Guard, the Berlin Wall, or open Communist encouragement of Arab aspirations to eliminate the infant nation of Israel (although it might legitimately be asked whether some or all of these are inescapably linked to the Marxist logic). Rather I am concerned with broader issues which, as you say yourself, are part and parcel of Marxist theory and practice.

Now, although it may not be the most important question we have to discuss, it does seem to me that at this point I must ask you to clarify the Marxist position in regard to religion. Here again it is not simply a question of what is happening in countries where the Communist party is in power—to Catholics in Czechoslovakia or to Jews in the Soviet Union—but rather a question of principle.

It is clear enough, I think, that "atheism" is a negative concept, and that no one need seriously concern himself with directly affirming this negation. The question, rather, is whether your affirmation of man's radical autonomy entails the elimination of religion, on the grounds that religion entails denying this radical autonomy. Is it inevitable that as a humanism Marxism must look upon religion as a dehumanizing, an "alienating" force? The question has nothing to do with the possibility or admissibility of persecuting religion; we can assume that this is not basic to Marxism. Rather, it is a question as to whether the advent of a positive, "scientific" socialism, such as Marx himself envisaged, entails as a logical result the disappearance of religion, which will simply cease to be a need of man. As a student of Marx (you know the texts as well as I do) I am convinced that Marx saw an absolute incompatibility between the advent of rational society and the continuance of religion, even as a phenomenon of individual consciousness.[1] You yourself constantly speak of religion as a form of "alienation," and since you say that alienation is a historical not a moral category,[2] this would seem to imply that whatever historical necessity you attribute to the advent of socialism you would also have to attribute to the disappearance of alienation and, hence, of religion. Is, then, your toleration of religion provisional, i.e. conditioned by your conviction that it will disappear through historical necessity, or do you foresee that my kind of religion and your kind of rationality can enduringly continue to exist side by side? Can you conceive of a religion which would not alienate? I am certainly prepared to admit that every instance of religion which in the concrete does thus alienate man is by that very fact a travesty of the true reality of religion and as such should disappear. But that is another question.

Garaudy:

It is first of all necessary to recall that the theoretical basis of Marxist socialism is not atheism but humanism, militant humanism, which is to say the struggle for the full development of man, of every man, against whatever would mutilate or impoverish him.

Marx himself did not like the term "a-theism," because, he said, it is a negative term. Socialism, then, cannot be defined as the negation of God but only as the affirmation of man.

Marxist atheism, then, is historically only a consequence of its humanism—when religion constitutes an alienation of man, i.e. when it deprives man of his autonomy, of his creative pride. Marx was writing in a Europe dominated by the "Holy Alliance," in which princes were united, for the defense of religion, against peoples struggling for freedom. Under these circumstances religion was "the opium of the people," used to justify the established disorder (under the pretext of "divine right") and to preach resignation to the oppressed.

Like Marx and Engels, Lenin was always opposed to inserting atheism into the statutes of the Communist party. On the subject of "the workers' party attitude toward religion" Lenin was of the opinion that even a priest had the right to belong to the Communist party. At the present time in France, Italy, and Spain, tens of thousands of Christians are militant members of various Communist parties. If, up to now, there are but few priests among them, it is their hierarchy which forbids them, not the Communist party.

These are the principles of Marxism in the matter.

Still, it is also true that in some socialist countries there have existed and still exist tensions in relation to the churches. The situation in no way derives from the principles of Marxism but from historical conditions, in particular from the connection of the churches with counterrevolutionary forces.

In the Soviet Union, for example, before the October Revolution the majority church, i.e. the Orthodox Church, was an instrument of the state. Not only was there a state religion, but this privileged Church, heir of an ancient Caesaro-Papist tradition of links with power—a tradition dating from the Byzantine Empire—with Czarist support persecuted other religions: Catholics and Uniates, Protestants, Jews, and Mohammedans.

The Socialist Revolution separated the Church from the State, and in its constitution it consecrated the right of practicing any religion whatever—or none at all.

The Orthodox Church, however, in its desire to preserve its ancient privileges, its huge feudal landed properties, and its position in the state, identified itself with the counterrevolutionaries, not only blessing their arms but often even taking part in their battles. The struggle against this kind of clergy was not an antireligious but a political struggle, as was that of the French Revolution against a clergy which had identified itself with feudalism and the monarchy.

At present, due above all to the patriotism manifested by the majority of the Orthodox clergy in the struggle against Hitlerism in World War II, the situation is constantly improving.

Other examples could be given, such as that of Poland. The fact that the Polish episcopate always voted in Vatican Council II with the conservative minority does not simplify relations between the Church and the Polish State.

On the other hand, in a country like Hungary, now that its Church is no longer under a feudal lord like Cardinal Mindszenty—who announced on Radio Budapest in 1956 that the land would be taken back from the peasants and returned to their former owners among the nobility, the relations between Church and State are returning to normal. Thanks to the concordat signed three years ago by the Vatican and the Hungarian State, archbishops and bishops have been appointed by the Pope in agreement with the State, and the Catholic Church—like other churches in that country—has its own journals, its own missions, its press, and the other means of expression which it needs.

In countries like France we are faced with a situation whose historical conditions are new. The attitude of hundreds of thousands of Christians and of a large number of priests sincerely attached to socialism is preparing the way to a march toward socialism side by side with Communists and other socialists, and this can imply no restriction on the liberty of faith.

Under conditions such as these a complete religious freedom is quite possible. It would be contrary to the principles of Marxism to substitute a state atheism for a state religion. The state should be neutral with regard to religion, which is a private matter.

Essentially the whole thing depends on the attitude of Christians themselves. No one should be disturbed because of his faith. We Marxists recognize no other criterion than loyalty with regard to the construction of socialism, and right now the historical proof of this is that believers can be just as militant as atheists. The construction of socialism, thus, is not a religious problem, and any persecution of faith would be contrary to the very principles of Marxist socialism.

Lauer:

It is quite clear to me that in the last twenty years the attitude toward religion has, externally at least, changed significantly in many Communist countries. It is clear, too, that both Marxists and Christians are entering more and more into serious dialogue. The question still remains, however, whether you can foresee the possibility of genuine and complete religious liberty within a Marxist framework. By "religious liberty" I do not mean the freedom to advocate a political or social structure which would simply cancel out all the gains which have been made in the direction of genuinely human growth and development. Religious liberty cannot mean the freedom to return to a feudal situation or to one of capitalist exploitation. But it does, in my opinion, mean the freedom not only to put one's beliefs into practice but also to express one's religious convictions even where this involves open criticism of social structures or of the Communist government's policies and activities. Do you honestly foresee this sort of liberty as a permanent possibility within a Marxist structure of society? Do you foresee the possibility that the Christian Church will be able to carry out its essential mission of preaching redemption through

Christ, without hindrance from the Communist regime? There may be a true sense in which one can say that religion is a "private matter," but there is an equally true and important sense in which the Christian religion cannot be a private matter: It is essentially apostolic and committed to speak out against any system which impedes the public expression of faith. After all, only if Communism can accept active Christianity as not antagonistic to its aspirations can Christianity accept Communism as not antagonistic to its aspirations.

This is not the place, it would seem, to dispute your somewhat naïve historical explanation of Communism's opposition to established religion—in the Soviet Union, for example. It is still curious that Catholics, Protestants, and Jews were persecuted by the same revolutionary party which you say was opposed only to the privileged Orthodox Church. I leave the accuracy of your statistics to the mercy of our well-informed readers. What is far more important is the question as to whether Marxist logic can accept any strong religious body. Can religion—particularly the Christian religion—do what it is supposed to do and not be considered a danger? It is simple enough to *say* that persecution of religion is contrary to Marxist principles; to what extent does Marxist practice follow these somewhat ill-defined principles? The fact is that Christians do not trust Communists. Should they? You seem to find it necessary to say that, where tensions exist, this is due to the counterrevolutionary activities of the Church. Do you mean that it is never due to the doctrinaire attitude of Marxists and their a priori conviction that religion can be only bad—unhistorical?

It is not that I experience any difficulty in understanding why Marxist "humanism" is opposed to Christian "theism." My difficulty rather is in understanding how it can remain what it is and not be seriously opposed to any belief in God. I may well be wrong, but it seems to me that your

way of thinking must inevitably be opposed to any acceptance of God. To accept God is to accept a being superior
to man and a reason which is essentially superior to merely
human reason. I can understand the fear engendered by
the very possibility that men might accept such a being
and such a reason; it is a fear shared by many atheistic
humanists who are not Marxists. Still, I can see no com-
pelling reason why any philosophical theory should take
such a hold on me that I cannot countenance anything
which might throw doubts on the all-embracing character
of the theory. If my faith does not square with my theory,
I can see reasons why my faith might need re-examining;
I can see no reason why the theory may not stand re-
examining. You have admitted that science and technology
cannot solve all the problems they raise; perhaps the dialectic cannot do so either. The fact is that the very fear I
mentioned seems to me to be an irrational fear. If human
reason is *de facto* a participation in divine reason, I do
not see that it is therefore any less reason or, for that
matter, any less autonomous. What *reasons* are there for
asserting that man's reason must be the only reason there
is, unless it be that you *will* that it be so? It might
actually be more rational to share Descartes' rational-
istic fear that human reason may be condemned ever to be
deceived—*if* there is no divine veracity to guarantee it.
On the other hand, I can understand your *will* that there
be only human reason; what I cannot do is recognize the
demand as "scientific." What reason is there to fear that
man will not be truly rational, if he is not the totality of
rationality, that he will not be truly creative, if he is not
the totality of creativity?

There may be very good reasons to hold suspect "timeless answers" to men's questions. Still, reasons to hold
suspect are not reasons (except arbitrarily a priori ones)
to deny the very possibility of timeless answers. Even the
affirmation that "religion is a human project"[3] does not

solve the problem (if any mere affirmation solves any problem). Of course religion is a human project, just as any human response, whether it be to the human or to the more-than-human, is a human project. Nor have you clinched the argument by asserting that "unlike scientific hypothesis [religion] does not submit to the criterion of practice,"[4] *unless* you are quite sure (a priori) that practice itself does not reveal the more-than-human which religion demands. Granted that "believers who are intimately involved in scientific activity see the vanity of the mythical explanation as soon as the scientific explanation has become possible."[5] They do not thereby become nonbelievers; in fact, it is precisely this confidence in rational explanation which strengthens their belief in the God who is not explanatory. No reasonable man wants a supernatural explanation, where a natural one is possible; but neither does any reasonable man see a conflict between the natural and the supernatural. Not only do we not minimize man by magnifying God; we magnify God by magnifying man. You may want to call this the "ontological argument"; to which all I can reply is, "So be it."

When we turn from the relation of science and religion, it is inevitable that we should come to the relation of Marxism and science. For the moment, however, we can leave aside any further discussion of the scientific character of Marxism itself—since that will concern us later—and concentrate on what we might call the Marxist (dialectical) character of contemporary science. It is quite obvious, of course, that, if a Marxist dialectical logic is the only logic valid for thinking a world which is in constant process, as Engels claimed, then all contemporary science is necessarily tributary to the Marxist way of thinking. The same holds, if what you say is true when you say that Marxism is "the *prise de conscience* of the profound movement of our history"[6]—although it is not clear what authorizes your use of the definite article "the" in your statement. Since, however, contemporary scientists are not aware of this, it would seem that it can be true only if the Marxist dialectic is a hidden presupposition of scientific thinking. You say, for example, that the cybernetic notion of "model" dominates scientific thinking today. This means, among other things, that scientists today are aware of the inevitably subjective character of their thinking and thus of the necessarily provisional character of their explanations and particularly of the formulations which express these explanations. Granted, then, that Marxist thinking lends itself readily to formulation in terms of this same notion of "model," it is still difficult to see that in this awareness scientific thinking owes anything to Marxism (rather than vice versa), unless the chronological priority of Marx is by itself an argument in favor of influence—and provided that the whole thing is not seen as a movement whose roots antecede Marx considerably and of which Marxism is only *one* of the provisional results. I say "provisional," because you seem to be saying that the Marxist dialectic is final, at least in the sense that all future thinking will have to be dialectical *in this way.*

Let us get back, however, to the notion of "model," since you do admit that a "plurality of models of socialism" is necessary.[7] I presume, then, that you cannot claim one of these models as uniquely valid for all future time. Now, unless you mean by "Communism" the generic name for the movement which is Communism by the very fact that it is valid, your logic would seem to force you to admit the possibility of a future model whose only resemblance to Communism will be that of counting Communism as one of the "moments" in its dialectical history. If this be true, however, how are we to interpret the following statement: "It is Communism alone, as Gorki wrote, which will create the true conditions of a society in which love will cease to be a promise, or a moral law, and will become the

objective law of the whole society"?[8] Apart from the
somewhat undialectical element of prediction in this
statement and its somewhat unintelligible description of
love as an "objective law," there are several questions
which, in the light of your previous remarks, it elicits.
(1) Granting that Communism may serve as a dialectical
moment in the advent of this utopian society, is it not
more than likely that the society itself will be *beyond*
Communism (unless, of course, "beyond Communism"
is meaningless)? (2) What justifies the statement
(Gorki's, which you make your own) that Communism
will do this "alone"? Taken literally, does not such a
statement effectively deny any real significance to dialogue? Or does the statement simply mean that this society will not be realized without the contribution of
Communism—which is historically verifiable, since Communism is already on the scene and is making its contribution? I ask the questions here, because on the answers
to them depends my partial agreement with another
statement of yours: "That which precisely constitutes the
philosophical revolution inaugurated by Marx is his having, for the first time, indissolubly linked theory and
practice, philosophical thought and militant action for
the transformation of the world, his having thus made
of theory a moment in the process of history taking
place."[9]

Garaudy:

You ask if it is possible for the Church to express its
faith, even if that implies criticizing the policies of the
socialist government. This I see as a particular instance
of a more general problem, which is to say that which
concerns the possibility of constructing a socialism which
involves a plurality not only of political parties but also
of spiritual families.

The problem will be examined later. Still, even at this stage of the discussion several remarks are in order.

First of all, the possibility you envisage is already a fact. In Poland, for example, the Church is not inhibited in multiplying its public attacks not only against the government but also against the regime itself. Now, difficulties do not arise from the fact that such criticisms are made but rather from the fact that they are criticisms made by a "conservative" Church, whose bishops at Vatican Council II always voted with the reactionary minority. It is a question, then, of a Church which is not particularly "open" to the modern world, which is oriented to the past. Still, even in this extreme case, without persecution of any sort, coexistence is a fact.

The question will be put in infinitely more favorable circumstances when we concern ourselves with a Christianity more open to the reality and to the aspirations of our times. In France, for example, there already exists among Christians—Catholic or Protestant—a very strong current, which takes its inspiration from the spirit of the Council, oriented toward a policy of progress in all areas. There we find Christians collaborating amicably with non-Christian unions in the struggle for social justice, in the struggle for peace, and against all forms of colonialism and neocolonialism, participating actively in the struggle for democracy and socialism.

In France there will be in the near future a decided majority in favor of socialism. This socialism will not be built by Communists alone, nor will it be only as the Communists imagine it or want it to be. Each of the participants in this common endeavor will bring to it its own original contribution, both critical and constructive. French Communists do not look upon this pluralism as simply a tactical necessity or as a "necessary evil," but rather as a source of enrichment for the very conception of socialism. Everyone has a different experience of the evil of the monopolistic capitalist system and, consequently, different aspirations in regard to the future. This future will be fully human only if it is symphonic.

Among the various advocates of socialism, then, there can be not only a factual coexistence and a mutual tolerance but also an emulation fruitful for all. It is not out of the question, for example, that Christians, who have always emphasized subjectivity and the interior life of the person—sometimes to excess, to the detriment of social commitment and of the historical and practical dimensions of life—will formulate demands which are happily complementary to those of Marxists, who for their part emphasize historical efficacy, at the risk of working for it unilaterally—not because they deny the role of subjectivity, which both Marx and Lenin stressed, but because they have a tendency to underestimate it.

When, for example, Marxists affirm that various alienations (economic, political, religious) have an historical character, that they have come into being as an historical moment and will disappear when the conditions which engendered them—in particular the mercantile system, wherein man exploits man—will have disappeared, we find that Christians look upon another alienation as more fundamental, inhering in man's very nature. What we have in common, despite this profound difference, is the will to put an end to all historical alienations, to all exploitation, oppression, mutilation, and humiliation of man. When we have done this together, if Marxists should be too quick to be satisfied (which would be contrary to the very principles of Marxism, whose dialectic implies endless development), and if vigilant Christians were there to remind them that the horizon always stretches beyond what has been realized, there would be an example of fruitful emulation and a happy complementarity.

On the other hand, it would be both deception and

self-deception if, under the pretext that any human realization is inadequate, imperfect, and incomplete, Christians were to be unwilling to accomplish together with
Marxists the primordial task of social transformation. In
this case religion would be unworthily utilized as an
acceptance or even justification of the established disorder. It would then constitute the doctrinal basis of a
policy of opposition not only to socialism but to every
step in the direction of the future. Historical examples of
this sort of attitude on the part of the churches are in-
numerable.

Even in such a situation, however, the Church should
not—no more than any other opposition movement—be
deprived of all means of expression. To accept, as does the
French Communist party, the principle of a plurality of
parties supposes the recognition of a right to criticism and
opposition.

It is clear, of course, that this right to criticism and
opposition is not a right of sabotage or armed rebellion,
or of an appeal to foreign forces. A socialism willed by the
majority of a people has not only the right but the duty to
protect its own accomplishments against sabotage and
subversion. The French Revolution of 1789 had to defend
itself against feudal uprisings, attacks by *émigrés*, and
foreign intervention. The October Socialist Revolution
had to defend itself against enterprises of the same sort
and was able to triumph over them only because the
masses did, with great heroism, defend the future against
the forces of the past.

Lauer:

Although there are a number of questions I asked to
which you have not responded, the remarks you did make
regarding significant religious liberty in countries dominated by the Communist party should, I think be helpful

in enabling us to come to an understanding. You say that
the kind of freedom I envisage is a fact—at least in Poland
—or that what opposition remains to Christianity is an
opposition to its reactionary and not to its religious
character. Here, I am afraid, I am simply not convinced.
The task of convincing the world that Christians enjoy
complete religious liberty in Poland is about as difficult
as that of proving to anyone that Jews enjoy complete
religious liberty in the Soviet Union. Really, it might be
better to stick with questions of principle and hope that
the facts will gradually catch up with them. In this regard
the example of French Communists is unquestionably
interesting, but it still proves only what can be expected
when Communists are *not* in power, when they are in the
minority.

For our purposes, however, we can, I think, confine
ourselves to the question of principle, which can be put
this way: Does Marxism today continue to look upon
religion as "essential alienation," so that to concede
religious liberty would eventually contradict its principles, or can it really envision a cooperation of completely
free partners in the struggle against all forms of alienation—whether under the form of a travesty of religious
principles or under that of a univocal conception of
socialism?

I asked the question at the outset, because the answer
to it conditions my agreement with you on a number of
positions which I know are yours. I can agree with you
only if I know that these positions do not involve the
conviction on your part of ultimate incompatability between what you seek and the enduring presence of religious faith in the society of the future. (1) I agree, for
example, that human work is not merely a means for
securing that which makes human living possible; it is
itself a humanizing force, an indispensable element of
human dignity, an integral factor in the progressive

realization of authentic humanity (though I see nothing wrong with its having the additional function of securing the wherewithal to make other human activities possible). What I do not see is that religious faith is a less significant humanizing force in the progress of man or that it in any way conflicts with the humanizing function of work. (2) By the same token I recognize that the kind of ownership of the means of production which effectively permits the few who own to control the lives of those who do not, is intolerable. (3) More than that, I admit that an economic, social, and political system which, since the days of the Industrial Revolution, has done relatively little toward eliminating ignorance, poverty, misery, suffering—in short, all the human ills which are not simply inseparable from the human condition (e.g. sickness and death)—should be seriously questioned and either remodeled or replaced. This does not mean, however, that I am convinced that you have found the *only* means for accomplishing that, or that I agree with your contention that only social revolution and not social reform can be valid as a remedy. (4) I can agree, too, that colonialism, whether directly political or purely economic (any system which makes a whole people dependent on another people—or on the industrialists among them), is not compatible with the dignity of man as man. Here, however, certain qualifications are necessary in order to avoid both historical and psychological naïveté: (a) "Colonialism" is not to be defined at the whim of the one who uses the term, so that it applies to the instances he does not like but not to the ones he approves (there can also be intolerable conditions of political independence); (b) territorial unity and, hence, national identity are very frequently matters of historical and geographical accident, which cannot be unmade simply by turning back the clock, and certainly not through the interference by outsiders in the internal affairs of a people; (c) nor can the question of national identity be settled by the mere fact of geographical separation, which again is arbitrary. With regard to this last, I have the utmost sympathy for aspirations to "national liberation"—in Asia, Africa, Latin America—but I know of no convincing a priori grounds for saying that this is always the only, or even the best, solution (even apart from the difficulty of determining just what constitutes the "nation" to be liberated).

There is one more point on which I am sure we must be in basic agreement: (5) that war, and particularly nuclear war, can in no sense serve as an instrument of human progress. We have reached the point in history where *every* nation must renounce war—or even the threat of violence—as a means of political action. The scandal of indefinite armament stockpiling, at a time when "two thirds of the children born into the world are condemned from birth either to a premature death or to invincible misery"[10] is a disgrace to humanity. This must be true everywhere, or it is true nowhere; and the excuse that it is the other fellow who wants war—thus making armaments necessary for defense—must end, or else the human race will.

Garaudy:

Permit me, Father, to interrupt you for a moment in regard to what you say about "the interference by outsiders in the internal affairs of a people." I detect in that another way of expressing one of the anti-Communist's favorite themes, that of "exporting revolution."

Among anti-Communists this slogan has a basic *raison d'être:* By claiming that every revolution in the world is the result of a conspiracy organized in Moscow, anti-Communism can hide the fact that class oppression and national oppression are becoming more and more intolerable to millions of people apart from any outside stimulus.

Do you really believe that the starving peasants of Northeast Brazil need a call from Moscow to drive them to rebellion against inhuman living conditions? You know well that in Cuba the revolutionary initiative took hold independently of the Communists, and that in that case the real "exporting" was of a counterrevolution at the time of the nefarious invasion attempt at the Bay of Pigs.

In Vietnam the "exportation of counterrevolution" is even more flagrant. President Eisenhower himself admitted that free elections would have given an overwhelming majority to Ho Chi Minh in the South as well as the North. This, he said, was the reason for not applying the Geneva agreements.

It is amusing, incidentally, to note that the precise reproach directed by Chinese leaders against the Soviet Union was the failure of the latter to "export the revolution." The Soviet position was that revolutions should develop "from within," as a result of the internal contradictions proper to each people, and that "peaceful coexistence" consists essentially in preventing at one and the same time the exportation of both revolution and counterrevolution.

Lauer:

Since, as a matter of fact, I did not say anything about "exporting revolution," I see no need of replying to you as though I did. What is more, I feel in no way constrained to take a position in favor of American political or military policy—as, I should hope, you do not regarding such policies in the Soviet Union, China, or even Cuba. Now that you have made your political point, I should like to get back to the question of religion.

I turn now to your evaluation, positive as well as negative, of Christian religion. Apart from a certain resentment at what I interpret as a pejorative sense and a rather patronizing manner in your use of such words as "myth" and "mystification," I see a real possibility in your thinking and in that of many contemporary Marxists—at least in Europe—of an understanding of religious aspirations which can be more than mere "tolerance" of human self-deception. I can even agree that a certain amount of "demythologizing" is in order, if Christianity is to measure up to its twentieth-century vocation (though I do not necessarily find the Bultmannian form of demythologizing the most authentically Christian). What I do not see is that "myth," in the way you understand it, alienates man in a way that "science" does not. You yourself speak of the "error which consists in believing that science and technology can solve all the problems which they themselves pose, thus neglecting the humanist moment of culture, that of seeking ends."[11] It is my contention that science itself becomes myth, when it seeks to solve problems outside its province or when it simply classifies them as illegitimate problems. It seems to me, however, somewhat arbitrary to insist on the "transcendent dimension" in man in this connection and then to call it "alienation," when this transcendence is interpreted as pointing beyond man, because it cannot be verified the way the purely human is verified. To say that you do not share the Christian experience is one thing; to say that those who do are "alienated" is another. It is my contention that the Christian experience is not only the encounter with God in Christ but that it is also an encounter with the total man in the same Christ. Thus Christianity, no matter what aberrations may mar its history, does not have to take a back seat to any "humanism" in its affirmation of man or in its insistence on human values. Nor do I see that either the example or the teaching of Christ failed to emphasize the social dimensions of love—even though we may find an unfortunate lack of emphasis on this dimension in much of what has historically called itself Christianity.

The point is, however, that it is thoroughly arbitrary to call the Christian's belief in transcendence an "alienation," on the ground that it is inseparable from his belief in God. Thus, I find no difficulty in granting that the call of God, be it in the Incarnation, the death of Jesus on the cross, or the Resurrection, finds its ultimate meaning deep within the subjective consciousness of the believer. This does not, however, mean that the call itself is no more than the projection of the believer's subjective need. The response to this call is a human decision, but it is not an alienation, any more than is any other authentic human response—unless it be the alienation of an arbitrarily demanded form of human autonomy, the belief in which is scarcely a rational exigency. Rather the response is, in my view, the realization of that which is more authentically human than mere postulated autonomy. Admitting, then, that the relation of the transcendent to man is meaningless apart from man's response and that, in this perspective, theology becomes a kind of (supernatural) anthropology, I cannot agree that this human response constitutes an "alienation" of the authentically human in man or a "mystification." To speak of theology as an anthropology is to recognize that, in reflecting on the human, one finds a transcendent dimension, which is not simply reducible to the natural or to an exigency which, when rationally considered, argues to an "absence" rather than to a "presence" of the divine. What is more, even if we admit that the form in which the divine call—and the human response to it—is translated may have to be reformulated at different levels of human culture (and history), no matter what the level, the call is a call to love—not, however, some isolated "love of God," which is not inescapably also a love of men. I cannot but think, however, that to see this divine-human love relationship as merely a phenomenon of human consciousness—worse still, of "imagination"—is at the very best arbitrary.

In all this I can recognize without hesitation that man's relation to God is not—cannot be—realized by his turning away from the world. This is the clear teaching of Jesus Christ himself, and to recognize it is but to reiterate the constant Christian paradox of a transcendence which is to be sought and found only in immanence. (I say "constant," even though historically it has frequently been obscured by a large dose of neo-Platonism in Christian thinking.) In this connection it may even be possible to translate Christian experience in your words and say that "transcendence is no longer an attribute of God but a dimension of man,"[12] provided that one can recognize in this dimension the more-than-human, the divine, in man— which does not mean that divinity simply becomes an attribute of man. For this reason I feel that, though it may be true to say that Marxist atheism differs from other atheisms in being able to integrate the valid aspirations of the believer, it is prejudicial to say that these aspirations "are found in a mystified (and thus, presumably, invalid) form in the believer."[13] What you seem to be saying is that Marxism can integrate religious aspirations, once they cease to be religious (which brings us back to the question as to whether you can "tolerate" religion, because you are quite sure that it will ultimately have the decency to disappear). Much the same problem is raised in my mind by another statement of yours that "transcendence is the alienated expression of culture's going beyond nature."[14] Simply to affirm that transcendence is transcended—demanded by your postulate of human autonomy—is not to transcend it.

There is no question in my mind that, in an age of scientific discovery, Christianity must, without becoming scientific—which is not its task—speak a language which does not contradict the legitimate claims of science. Thus, although I think we must both agree that Teilhard de Chardin was not a professional theologian, I can accept without hesitation the three requirements he demands of a modern theologian and which you cite:[15] "(1) The elimination from theology of all that is still linked to an archaic conception of the world. Revelation occurred at a time when the cosmos was still thought of as a finite and static whole. (2) The definition of the relationship between God and the world in a world which is conceived as a living organic totality, in ceaseless evolution and creation. (3) The elaboration of a theology which fully recognizes the value of work and of human effort, of scientific research as well as technical invention." I doubt, in fact, whether any respectable contemporary theologian would find fault with these requirements. I go even further—here at the risk of running afoul of the theologians—and assert with Teilhard that we are faced with the necessity of rethinking and reformulating the Christian doctrine of original sin (which is not to say that I refuse to recognize the reality of sin and fault or that I find the reality of man debased—"alienated," if you will—by such a doctrine). Both of us must recognize, I think, that man has in the past been unfaithful to his own basic (historical) orientation and that such infidelity always remains a human possibility in the future. If sin and fault are to be explained, then, they must be explained historically—and not as some sort of metaphysical inroad which makes man less than authentically human. Where I differ from you is that, while I see man's orientation and his task as essentially historical, I see the roots of this in the more-than-man in man and not merely in a history divorced from God, no matter what man's responsibility for that history may be. On the other hand, I admit that, to the extent that any Christian sees all this in terms of an orientation which is simply given from without, one which is not historical, not inner-directed, he is at fault. It is for this reason that I can endorse your statement: "Seen in this perspective, Christianity does not rule out but actually implies militant effort turned towards the future and its construction."[16] To teach anything less today would be infidelity to the Christian message. What I do not see, however, is that this teaching ceases to be true if God enters the picture, that the autonomy of man is in any way endangered by the presence of God. On the contrary, I find "militant effort turned toward the future and its construction" meaningless without God. Here I must agree with Father Rahner as you quote him:[17] "The experience of God is required for an integral humanism." As I see it, to experience man without experiencing God is not to experience man in his integrity. On the other hand, I am quite prepared to admit that, to the extent that capitalism (or any "system") renders such an integral humanism impossible, it cannot be supported by Christians. What is more, even prescinding from a direct condemnation of capitalism, which is not the point here, there can be no question that any genuine Christian must condemn the kind of pressure exerted by "Christian" industrialists who withdraw their financial support of Christian academic institutions as soon as the latter permit a kind of teaching which can be interpreted as critical of capitalism. If Christianity has to die of malnutrition, because there are no more wealthy industrialists to support it, then it deserves to die. It is a pretty weak faith in Christianity which sees this as a possibility—or worries about it.

III   MORAL PROBLEMS

Garaudy:

Rather than reply directly to your remarks concerning the question of principle in the Marxist attitude toward religion in general and toward Christianity in particular, I should like to turn to Marxism's concrete expectations when it looks at Christianity today.

With regard to the formation and development of norms for a public morality, what the non-Christian expects of the Church is necessarily a function of Christianity's image as it comes across to him now, as we approach the end of the twentieth century, in the attitude of the Church itself, its theologians, and the community of Christians.

As I see it, the most striking characteristic of Christianity in our times is that it is a Christianity on the march.

To say, then, what we expect, what we hope, from this Christianity is to attempt first of all to describe the transformations we are witnessing. This means tracing out the direction which we think we can discern in this advance and imagining the prolongation of this trajectory in a direction which we are not satisfied merely to wait for but which we hope for with all our heart, since we believe that on this orientation depends, to a great extent, the possibility of realizing in common the highest vocation of man.

One of the most positive results of the Council has been to encourage the development of a theology of earthly values which makes man the focal point of its preoccupations.

This orientation expresses a unified movement of Christianity, Protestant as well as Catholic, in the second half of the twentieth century.

The elaboration of a new, specifically Christian, humanism has been made possible by a profound reflection on transcendence.

The turning point, it seems to me, came with Karl Barth, who struck a decisive blow against dogmatism in theology. We could compare this critical aspect of Barth's work to Kant's "Copernican revolution" in philosophy. To all theological dogmatism, i.e. any attempt by the theologian to put himself in God's place and to speak in His name, Barth opposes the very principle of critical thinking: Whatever we say about God, it is men who say it.

This consciousness of radical discontinuity poses the problem of transcendence in its most exacting form: God is truly the "totally other." We do not find Him as the term of our reasoning or of our system of values. We have neither language nor morality in common with Him. The false dilemma of Plato's *Euthyphro* has been eliminated: "Is an act good because God has willed it?" asked Socrates, "or did God will it because it is good?" It was a confusion of God's word and man's word, a pretense of catching in the net of reason the initiative of God. The ultimate attempt along this line was that of Hegel who, in the last analysis, made of God the totality of human history and at the same time made of human history a false history, simply the unfolding—seemingly temporal— of a pre-existent totality, that of the Spirit. This was at one and the same time to diminish God, in order to adjust Him to this or that historical stage of reason, and to diminish man by taking from him his limitless possibilities of renewal and of creation.

In his commentary on the Epistle to the Romans, Barth reiterates, in opposition to Hegel, "what Kierke- gaard called the infinite qualitative distinction between time and eternity." In this way the rights of both God and man are completely protected. It is only if God is truly God, the "totally other," strictly transcendent, that man can be fully man. If there is continuity between God and man, all that is given to one is necessarily taken away from the other. If, on the contrary, there is no common measure between God and man, then history becomes a creation the total responsibility for which falls on man. Then, too, in a radical initiative, which nothing in man either prefigures or calls for—unless it be the negation of man's self-sufficiency—God can come toward man without limiting either his responsibility or his creative power.

This problem is met head on by Christian theologians and philosophers when they reflect on the challenge which atheistic humanism issues to faith.

In his remarkable book *El christianismo no es un humanismo*, Father González Ruiz puts strong emphasis on the "gratuity" of the Biblical God: On the cognitive level He is not an immanent answer to human problems; on the level of action grace does not interfere with na- ture. Only then is God not a rival to man's creative energy.

Father Ruiz condemns two errors in this regard. There is the error of having grace intervene in the sphere of immanence to the point of looking for a religious response to scientific, technical, moral, or political problems—which would be to misunderstand the autonomy of human values. There is a further error in accepting an "inflation of transcendence," which would place all authentic values beyond this world, thus making of human history a matter of no importance which spirit must bypass if it is to realize its vocation.

In both cases atheistic humanism, Marxist humanism, is right in considering the conception as one which paralyzes human effort.

The Council distinguished two essential accusations made by atheistic humanism:

1) Religion puts in question the autonomy of man.

2) Eschatological experience is an impediment to the full flowering of man in history.

There seems to be no question that, historically speaking, Christianity deserves to be accused on both counts. The problem, however, is not that of a polemic directed to the past but rather of determining whether it is essential to faith to play this alienating role.

Father González Ruiz proposes the following thesis: "Grace is not an intrusion which is to eclipse the epic grandeur of Prometheus" (p. 31). "The humanism which we are analyzing," he writes, "declares itself atheistic because it thinks that the Promethean vocation of man is incompatible with the recognition of God" (p. 23). Paul Ricoeur formulates a bold reply, based on a profound comprehension of the Bible: "Unlike Greek wisdom, Christianity does not condemn Prometheus. For the Greeks the fault of Prometheus was that of having stolen the fire of technology and of the arts, the fire of knowledge and of consciousness. Adam's fault is not the fault of Prometheus, his disobedience does not consist in being technical and scientific man; rather it is to have broken in his human adventure the vital link with the divine."

Father González Ruiz adds that "the readmission of Prometheus to the Christian calendar can be accomplished only after serious reflection on the biblical God." The problem is important, for what the contemporary humanist awaits and hopes for from Christianity is essentially this complete rehabilitation of Prometheus.

This is the path that Father Ruiz has resolutely taken, thus helping to demolish a major obstacle to the dialogue between Christians and Marxists. He writes: "The divine presence in the evolution of the world and of man is totally gratuitous: it cannot be perceived other than by God's own express revelation."

In opposition to a "deism manipulated by the interests of a dominating class," thus making of God "part of the cosmic and social system," Father Ruiz notes that "this stop-gap God recedes in proportion as man illuminates by his own progress the dark areas of ignorance and impotence. . . . The retreat of this 'God' is an indispensable condition for man's ascent—since God has become man's rival." On the basis of these two principles, "the uselessness of the God-hypothesis for explaining the problems of man, and the power of auto-creation in man's own effort, it is possible to offer humbly to the world the service of evangelisation."

"A Christianity which is disposed to struggle against every form of religious alienation," he continues, "can put no obstacle in the way of an integration, by common effort, of the upward movement of human activity" (p. 122).

"It is man who has the task of producing history by a constant effort to realize himself fully and to humanize nature. Thus we can understand that, in biblical religion, man's religious dimension should be precisely his complete and total responsibility for this humanizing evolution of the cosmos" (p. 33).

According to Father Chenu, in his Preface to the book,

this "theology of the world" served as material for the construction of the text on the pastoral constitution of the Church.

Starting from there we can judge the importance of the step which the Church is about to make, and we can speak of the hopes we can base on it.

The possibility of this humanism is born of the recognition that earthly values are autonomous.

The autonomy of science: God, according to Father Dubarle's witty remark, is not the little supplement to our mental deficiencies. Even though morality *can* intervene for the purpose of defining a hierarchy of urgency in planning research and *should* intervene for the purpose of judging the human values involved in applying science to the service of man's development or destruction, it must not intervene—no more than theology—in the free unfolding of the research itself.

Autonomy and value proper to action directed to the transformation and humanization of a world which, in turn, has its own proper, autonomous value: The optimism of Teilhard de Chardin in regard to what the world can become through the efforts of man, his exaltation of work, of technology, of scientific research, foreshadows Father Chenu's "theology of work." The latter writes: "Work continues the work of the Creator, and, through workers, God continues to be present in the world by transforming it."

Thus, man and man's world come, in post-conciliar theology, to the center of the Christian's preoccupations. "The question of man," says Father Rahner, "constitutes the whole of dogmatic theology."

The objection will be raised, perhaps, that such an attitude is not absolutely new in Christianity. That is true. In fact, however, this orientation towards man and the world has often been obscured in Christian thought by Greek dualism, which reigned almost uninterruptedly from the fourth to the twentieth centuries, making of Christianity that which Nietzsche called with justified scorn, "a Platonism for the people."

To teach that this world is not the essential, that "true life is elsewhere," beyond life and history, was to make of Christianity, as Rimbaud put it, "the eternal robber of human energies," or, according to Marx, "the opium of the people." This was encouraging not the effort to transform the world but rather disdain for the earth and resignation to all the iniquities of this "vale of tears," where man was to pass but a short time while waiting for a "beyond."

It is true that the Biblical God knew no spiritual realm separated from the earthly realm. It is true that it is Stoic philosophy and not the Bible which exalted an "interior" liberty, separated from the exterior, material, conditions of liberty. But it is also true that, in the history of Christianity, it is rare to hear a call to transform the world first in order to create the material conditions for spirituality. When the call was sent out it was condemned as heresy—from the "Circumcellions" to Thomas Münzer. When, outside the Church and in opposition to it, revolutions were undertaken to humanize man's world by putting an end to ancient privileges and ancient injustices, they were invariably condemned as diabolical—from the French Revolution of 1789 to that of 1848, from the Paris Commune to the October Revolution.

Scarcely ever before the second half of the twentieth century—and even then often with much timidity—has there been the beginning of a realization that "spiritualism" is the heresy which has given birth to the worst divisions between the Church and men.

In the effort to dissociate Christianity from traditional dualism Father Laberthonnière was a precursor. In this regard it is significant that his short, incisive essay "Christian Realism and Greek Idealism" was re-edited with a flourish after the Second Vatican Council. Confirming this sort of research, in order to dissociate Christianity from the Greek heritage—that of Plato and Aristotle as well as that of the Stoics and of Plotinus—Leslie Dewart, a Catholic philosopher, attempts in his book *The Future of Belief* to generalize the effort to distinguish what is fundamental in faith from the institutional or cultural forms of religion.

A similar movement is developing in Protestant thought. Ever since Karl Barth taught the present generation of theologians that religion is frequently the last battlefield where man wars against God and endeavors to make of God something less than the sovereign of life in its entirety, it has been the very notion of "religion" (to the extent that it opposes to this world "another world") which has been called into question in the name of faith. Dietrich Bonhoeffer had begun to speak of a "Christianity without religion," and Paul Ricoeur, a Protestant philosopher, could define religion as "alienation of faith."

To this movement toward disengaging what is fundamental in faith from the cultural forms which religion has put on at various stages of its historical development belong the investigations directed to the "demythologization" of faith inaugurated by Bultmann with his *Kerygma and Myth.*

There is no contesting, of course, the dominating idea which determines that faith be expressed in both language and forms of thought which correspond with the conception of the world and the philosophy proper to an epoch and to a society. What is more, certain Catholic critics of Bultmann, such as Fathers Malevez or Caffarena, have with good reason put this question: Is not myth necessarily the language of the kergyma? If it is true that the *concept* expresses and determines an already existing reality, is it not also true that myth is the expression of a reality which does not yet exist, that it is the language of promise and of call?

If, however, man can express this call of transcendence only in the language of myth, of art, and of poetry, how can he make clear this intervention of God?

The initiative, Barth teaches, can come only from God. But how recognize it? Far too long the intervention of God has been situated only in the lacunae in the web of natural causality, in miracles, or else in the gaps of our rationality, in the failures of our power or of our will. When will we, asked Bonhoeffer, look for God not in the insufficiencies, the miseries, the weaknesses of man, but at the frontiers of the human, at the forefront of human creation, in the plentitude of man's powers, in his grandeur and his joy?

If man meets God only in the world, if the world is the sole theater of this dialogue between God and man, if it is true that the Biblical God manifests Himself only in history, i.e in human actions, in victories or defeats, exiles or revolutions, if the word of God is always an act, and if God calls men in and through the happenings of social transformation, can we not then say that God is wherever something new is in the process of coming to life, wherever a new grandeur is given to the human form? This may be in scientific or technical discovery, in artistic creation and in poetry, in the liberation of a people or in a social revolution—wherever man becomes more like the image of God, a creator, and at every level of creation, whether that be in the economic or political order, on the level of scientific invention, or in the realm of the artistic or the spiritual.

Is not God present in all that is not the mechanical prolongation of the past, its result and its product; is He not present in that which transcends the past and brings it to fruition?

Attempts to eliminate from transcendence whatever could make of it a vestige of primitive superstitions lead man to interiorize the vital experience of transcendence as "the effort to transcend human limits with the help of God," as Carson Blake put it at the Ecumenical Council of Heraklion.

Transcendence, then, becomes a dimension of each creative act of ours. "Each consciousness," writes Bishop Robinson, "conceives the divine when it reflects on the operations by which it is constituted as consciousness."

For a Marxist, man is never the simple result or product of the past and of present conditions but something more which both sums up and exceeds this past and these conditions. Can he not, then, integrate this conception of transcendence—which is, after all, a fundamental dimension of man and not an attribute of God—by using the expression "dialectical progress beyond" to designate the moment of initiative and creation to which Christianity has always given the name "transcendence," in referring to the flowering or emergence of the divine in man's activity?

Is it not, then, the primary task of the Church to distinguish the "signs of the time," which is to say, the signs which point to God's presence and activity in the world, and to follow Him where He is?

Perhaps what unbelievers expect of the Church is that she should judge men, as well as political and social regimes, less on the basis of their attitude toward the Church and more on the basis of their attitude toward man.

Is the Church's mission to defend the Church or to defend man? This is not an abstract, purely theoretical question; it is an immediately concrete and practical one.

What has happened up to the present gives the impression that the Church has judged men, political programs, and regimes on the basis of their attitude in regard to the Church, according to the place in their state which they give to the Church. There is silence regarding the crimes of Franco, provided he respects or even extends the traditional privileges of the Church. Too often defense of the Church takes precedence over the defense of man. So true is this that the Church is always on the side of those who defend her, even if this defense is a means of crushing man; always against those who oppose her, even if this opposition is a necessary condition for the liberation of man. It is as though the Church were an end in itself and not a means of making hope real.

When a very high-ranking prelate exalts genocide in Vietnam, there is not a single official voice in the Vatican to condemn him unambiguously. To do this, we are told, would violate tradition or the rules of diplomacy. Well, why does not the Church stop being traditional and diplomatic and become prophetic?

Why does she not say to those who would turn a colonialist war into a crusade what Abraham Lincoln replied to a group of chauvinist priests: "Never say that God is on our side; let us pray rather that we may be on God's side"?

It is not inconceivable that God should be on the side of the very ones who deny Him, that they may be the ones who are contributing to a realization of God's revolution in the world. When, as we read in Isaiah (ch. 45), God turns to Cyrus, King of Persia, for the accomplishment of His plan, he does not choose one of those who call themselves servants of Jahweh. To go beyond this Biblical parable with its historical limitations, can we not say that God reveals Himself as the sort of explosive force which is expressed in a social revolution or in a struggle for national liberation? Is not God present wherever a group of men struggles to make of each man a center of initiative and responsibility, a creator in the image of God?

It is impossible, then, to acclaim God in a Portugal where fascist terror reigns, a Portugal which is waging the last overtly colonialist war against Angola—even if its government does honor the Virgin Mary. On the other hand, perhaps it *is* possible to acclaim God in Cuba, where in the space of three years not only the exploitation of man but also prostitution and illiteracy have been eliminated, whereas centuries of colonial servitude sanctioned by religion have perpetuated all three in the rest of Latin America. Perhaps Cuba is the real seat of the struggle to make of each man a man; perhaps there the work of God is being accomplished—even if a few Francoist priests are exiled in the process.

Why should God always be on the side of "the establishment" and never on the side of change?

Why should the Church not bear greater witness to its prophetic mission by showing itself capable of standing up to Mussolini or Hitler, even though this might call for massive martyrdom, instead of reserving its thunderbolts for those who love the future and know how to take risks for its sake?

This conservative social attitude has constantly been accorded weighty justification by the traditional interpretation of sin.

Here again the influence of Greek conceptions in transforming Biblical teaching has played an important role. It is as though the Christian notion of sin had been contaminated by the Greek notion of *hybris*, unbridled pride. This notion, incidentally, has lost in the process two important aspects given to it by Hellenic humanism: (1) In Greek tragedy *hybris* brings about the downfall of the arrogant man who opposes the will of the gods, but it is a sign of the hero's grandeur that he has entered into combat against destiny, in a battle which is lost from the start; (2) in addition, in the transition of Greek civilization from one epoch to another the rebellious hero is the bearer of the future's values—like Prometheus or Antigone.

There again greatness is found in transgression.

Now, in the traditional conception of sin the images of protest and revolt hold a central position, minus the counterpoise contained in the tragic grandeur of rebellion.

Most often pride is presented as the sin *par excellence:* Sin is a refusal to keep one's proper place. The Biblical myth is interpreted in this fashion. Sin is the violation of an order which imposes on man prohibitions and limits: Curiosity to know becomes culpable concupiscence of the spirit; man's sexual maturation becomes the concupiscence of the flesh; the vivifying passion to master nature and to dominate the human world becomes the temptation of Lucifer.

Are there not, as the American theologian Harvey Cox has suggested, political reasons for this centuries-old tendency to identify sin with insubordination?

When in the fourth century—with Constantine—Christianity becomes the dominant ideology and provides its sanction to the imperial authority and to the social hierarchy of which the latter is the summit, and again, when this fateful identification of the established order with an order willed by God will have held sway for more than a thousand years, sin, to quote Teilhard de Chardin, will be "an explanation of evil in a conception of the world as fixed."

In a perspective such as this the supreme fault, evil itself, is the disruption of this order. By the same token, piety implies the acceptance of this order.

It is not at all surprising, then, that at times of great social upheaval—in the Renaissance or after the French

Revolution—it is the rebels who are the most attractive heroes, those who make the head and heart of man leap: Milton's Lucifer, Goethe's Mephistopheles or Shelley's Prometheus breaking his chains.

In the nineteenth century every appeal to man's greatness begins with a challenge to Christianity; whether it be Kierkegaard who considers the only true sin to be "the despairing refusal to be someone," or Marx teaching that the social order is not a given but a task for man to accomplish—with its necessary corollary that religion is the opium of the people—or Nietzsche proclaiming that a God who does not permit man to be a creator ought to be killed.

Thus for five centuries—since the pre-Renaissance period and the disintegration of the feudal world—there has been an ever increasing divorce between man's aspirations to autonomy and the traditional teaching of the Church.

Burckhardt has shown that medieval man had no consciousness of himself except as an element of a whole, as part of an order, as member of a community. The decisive turning point in modern history comes when the individual can think of himself as an autonomous reality, not apart from his social relationships, but also not reduced to the sum total or to the result of those relationships. Has the Church been able to reach this turning point?

One could ask whether the traditional conception of sin has not continued to be, to a certain extent, the metaphysical expression of the social order which dominated the West from Constantine to the fifteenth century.

Can we not also consider the concern with realizing a new meeting of the Church and the world as a principle unifying the diverse theological endeavors which preceded and followed Vatican II?

From this point of view have not nonbelievers reason

to expect of the Church that it will, in the framework
of this new perspective, rethink the notion of sin, with a
view to interpreting it in a manner more in accord with
the spirit of our times?

In his *Christology and Evolution* Teilhard de Chardin
was already moving in this direction. On the Protestant
side, taking his cue from Bonhoeffer, Harvey Cox is of
the opinion that sin is not so much doing what should
not be done as it is not doing what should be done. In
Biblical tradition, he says, sin is man's abdication and refusal of responsibility. The paradigmatic fault is that of
Eichmann, whose invariable defense at his trial was: "I
was carrying out the orders of the Führer." Sin, then, consists in being in an alienated society and acting the
part of a marionette put in motion by that society's structures. It means accepting as models of conduct stereo-
types imposed from without, letting oneself be carried
along by events. In a word, sin is not wishing to be
more than a man, it is accepting to be less than a man.

Due to this historical conditioning and the theological
backwardness consequent on it, the present situation has
resulted: Christians do not know how to live in a revolution.

Does this mean that Christians lack a theology of revolution? It is not for me to judge this, although there are
precedents, in a Thomas Münzer, for example, a John
Hus, or the English "Levellers."

The common denominator of the Christian revolution
—or of a revolutionary Christianity—is perhaps that of
having taken seriously the prayer which asks God that
His will "be done on *earth* as it is in heaven."

Loisy said of the first Christian generations: "They
awaited the Kingdom, and it was the Church which
came." This sort of thing is illustrated in the militant mil-
lenniarism of Münzer, where Christians set themselves

not only to hope for the Kingdom but to fight for its realization: "In its original principle," said Münzer, "faith gives us impossible things to accomplish, the realization of which the delicate could not imagine." He affirmed two essential themes in his theology of revolution: first, that of applying the force of faith to the real transformation of the world with a view to the full realization of man; secondly, never forgetting to orient this renovation of earthly life to a higher finality. In this perspective faith is no longer opium but rather a ferment of man's continuous creation of the world and an opening of human history toward an infinite horizon.

If it is true of every man that God created him a creator, is not a Christian's primordial task in the world that of struggling against all forms of "alienation," which degrade man by making of the subject an object? In our time this has a concrete significance: that of putting an end to the proletarian condition which turns each worker into a means rather than an end, a means of producing surplus value. It also means putting an end to all forms of colonialism or neocolonialism which prevent millions of men from achieving the dignity of being artisans of their own destiny; it means putting an end to an armaments race and to latent or virtual war whose effect is to compel each people to devote to the possible destruction of man the wealth and power which could give to millions the possibility of achieving a properly human dignity, that of being cultured, responsible and creative.

The concrete struggle against these alienations (i.e. against all that prevents millions of men from being men, creators in the image of God) can and should become the strongest link of solidarity between Christians and Marxists.

Marxists should not forget what they owe, on this level, to Christian teaching.

Greek humanism discovered and elaborated an aspect

and an essential moment of freedom, i.e. necessity and the
knowledge of necessity. The highest freedom, in this
view, is necessity understood. In the Hellenic conception
of the world and of man the idea of creation is absent.

In the Judaeo-Christian conception, on the contrary,
creation is primary, and man's freedom is not defined
as consciousness of necessity but as participation in the
creative act. The New Testament announces this "good
news": At each moment man can begin a new future, can
master the laws of nature and of society. Christ's resurrection is the paradigm of this new freedom: Death itself,
the limit *par excellence*, which defines our inexorable
finitude, has been conquered.

This lived experience of the possibility of escaping the
"given" world and inaugurating a new future is the experience of a double transcendence: God's radical transcendence in relation to man is the foundation of man's
transcendence in relation to nature, to society, and to
his own history.

If man is more than the necessary product of nature's
laws and society's structures, more than the prolongation
and result of his past, he can exercise his right to overcome necessity only if he shares in the very activity
whereby the world is continually being created.

It is for Marxists to recognize the importance of this
Christian contribution not only to their cultural but also
to their militant heritage.

That too, however, gives them the right to expect of the
Church a new dynamism.

Unlike the first Adam, who committed the original sin
of letting his conduct be dictated from without, of sur-
rendering himself to the dictates of a serpent, the second
Adam, Jesus, affirmed man's prerogative, that whereby
he is definitively raised above the rule of nature. Is it
not the essential message of Jesus to have shown that
the forces which rule in the world do not have the power

to determine man, that man can make himself independent in relation to any destiny? This means that no economic forces, no class relationships, no instinctual or physiological drives, no psychological or moral pressures of the family, class or nation, no structural exigency of nature or society, can completely determine him, even though all these in large measure condition his actions and his thoughts.

Is not the essential message of Jesus this message of transcendence, of man's dialectical passage beyond the confining tyranny of forces both intrapersonal and suprapersonal?

When is the Church going to remind us, in its day-by-day activity, that the exigency which God has brought to our attention by the "gesture" of Christ is the defatalization of history and the disalienation of man?

In this last third of the twentieth century, what unbelievers expect first of all from the Church is that she give back to the message of Jesus its power of breaking with the given.

Such a message from the Church presupposes, to begin with, that the accent be put less on personal piety and the interior life of the spirit, more on the historical and social dimension of love.

Amid the disorder of a thinking which endeavors to raise itself to the level of actuality, i.e. the gigantic metamorphosis taking place in the twentieth century, here, then, are some reflections on what non-Christians expect of the Church along the lines of an elaboration and development of norms for a public morality.

This comes down, ultimately, to three precise demands:

1) To recognize the autonomy of human values, cognitive and practical.

2) To accept man's Promethean ambition to create continually both the world and himself.

3) To decide clearly to "give clearance" to both the word and the reality, *socialism*, a condition for the limitless development of man and of all men.

We await with anxiety and with hope that these steps be taken, because our common future depends on it. No Christian is asked to be less a Christian; rather each is asked to be more fully Christian, i.e. to be able to give a Christian answer to the problems of our times and to give it in the spirit of our times.

For we are profoundly certain of this: Communism will not be able to succeed fully until it has integrated into the image of man what is best in the Christian contribution—but this integration will not be possible until fundamental Christian values are no longer obscured by a conservative policy in the Church.

Lauer:

It is difficult for me to determine whether I should reply directly to your last remarks or whether I should simply make a counterproposal and speak of what the Christian expects of Communism. My fear, however, is that this latter course might involve me in the sort of historical indictment which we both agreed at the outset would serve no purpose in our present endeavor. There are a number of things that Christians would like to see Communism stop doing—whether it be impeding the free movement of its people, prosecuting the free expression of its intellectuals, or insisting that social revolution is valid only when it is Communist in form—but that is not the point. What the Christian wants to see is something positive, i.e. that the logic of Marxist theory really is oriented to the genuine betterment of man and that

Communist practice is more concerned with the good of human beings throughout the world than it is with expanding its own sphere of influence. It is inevitable, of course, that a theory which sees political action as inseparable from the endeavor to bring about a socialistic form of society should be constantly motivated by political considerations in its endeavors. It remains true, however, that political action or political influence can only be a means related to a more significant end which is man himself. What the non-Communist fears is that emphasis on the means can result in losing sight of the end or in making the means the end. At the very least, I think, present-day Marxist propaganda leads to the belief that such fears are justified.

What I really seek, then, is the kind of mutual understanding which will permit both Marxists and Christians to pursue more effectively what is positive in each one's commitment. With a view to this I shall address myself to the points you have just made, with a hope that in so doing I shall also be getting across some of my own reactions to Marxism.

This seems all the more apropos since in your remarks I discern the expression of your principal objection to the Catholic Church, i.e. its inadequate concern with the needs of mankind as a whole, its concentration on the "spiritual" needs of its own children and, consequently, its seeming indifference to the continued advantages which the privileged enjoy over the underprivileged. Your objections, incidentally, indicate somewhat indirectly the reasons for the Church's continued opposition to Marxist socialism—even though its attitude is far less unsympathetic than it has been in the past.

Before I go on, however, I must clear up a possible misunderstanding to which your position could give rise. When we began our "Christian-Communist" discussions we both, I think, agreed that neither of us could claim

to be thoroughly representative of one or the other side
in the controversy. Still, we felt that we should be even
less representative, if either of us were to adopt a particularist point of view. Now, it seems to me that, by
directing the bulk of your objections against the "official"
position of the Roman Catholic Church, you are putting
me in the particularist position of engaging in a *Catholic-*
Communist" and not a *"Christian-*Communist" dialogue.
If I were to put you in the position of representing only
Soviet Communism, you could, I think, legitimately object. By the same token I cannot agree that for me to
represent a Christian—or even a Catholic—position involves my denying that some of the Church's hierarchy
and even the Vatican are capable of adopting a position
which is scarcely recognizable as Christian. It may be, of
course, that I simply must put up with the inconvenience
in discussion of being on a side which boasts not only an
identifiable central authority but also a long history,
whereas you stand on the side of no indentifiable authority and a short history. What must be clear is that in
standing up for what I consider to be Christian principles
I consider it both my right and my obligation to oppose
what I consider un-Christian, whoever it may be who by
his words or his actions shows himself to be un-Christian.
It is my hope that you enjoy the same freedom to repudiate what in the concrete does not measure up to the
principles for which you stand.

In any event, when you tell us what atheistic humanism—which for some unassignable reason you make
synonymous with Marxist humanism—expects from the
Church, I can be most grateful. At one and the same
time you provide a background against which Christian consciousness can come to an awareness of its own
concrete defects and you describe an attitude toward
man and society, many elements of which Christianity
can well make its own. Since, however, even a valid

description of what Christianity *should be* does not constitute a description of what Communism *is,* I do not feel constrained to agree either that Marxist humanism is preferable to Christian humanism or that, if Christianity is to break with its relatively conservative past, it should align itself with precisely the form of socialism you advocate. Nor is it legitimate to imply that the Church is opposed to Communism because it is opposed to the end of social justice which you claim to be the goal of the Marxist ideal of social revolution. There are enough other reasons for it to be opposed to Communism. Throughout your remarks I discern a tendency to confuse the question of fact, e.g. the Church's opposition, and the question of value, e.g. the reasons for that opposition.

Although I am prepared to admit that the "social teaching of the Church" frequently leaves something to be desired, it is not, I am convinced, a defect in this teaching which prompts it to refuse its blessing to Communism. Nor is it mere concern with the preservation of its own privileges—or even its own existence—which prompts it to look with a jaundiced eye at Communism's perennial opposition to religion. The value of religion is independent of any privileges it may enjoy. What is more, when one looks at the attitudes of Marx, Engels, and Lenin toward religion, it is difficult to look upon opposition to religion as merely accidental to the ideology you represent, or as justified by the weaknesses you discern in the official Vatican position.

The Church can scarcely condemn Communism because it resorts to violence, but there are types of violence which seem endemic to Communism and which the end in view scarcely justifies. It is customary, I know, since the Twentieth Party Congress, to say that Communists universally repudiate Stalinism. It is significant, however, that the repudiation of Stalin dates from the period after Stalin's death, not from the time when the aberrations

of Stalinism should have been manifest to any thinking
man. It is understandable, of course, that no one in the
Soviet Union should previously have had the courage
openly to condemn Stalin, but it is somewhat less than
edifying to find in Communist ranks no prophetic voice
even at a great distance willing to say unequivocally what
became the mode, once the Twentieth Party Congress
gave the signal. Were it not so tragic it would be amusing
to read in the Appendix to the Acts of the Twentieth
Party Congress[1] words of complete approval from Mau-
rice Thorez and Palmiro Togliatti, who but a short time
before were untiring in speaking of "the great Stalin." One
wonders, incidentally, if one can secure such unanimity
of opinion as was evidenced throughout the Congress
from men or only from robots. I am prepared to admire
an ability to recognize that one has been wrong—whether
it be a Togliatti, a Thorez, or a Roman Catholic bishop
who does so—but I cannot but be amazed when such a
universal about-face is accomplished in so short a time.

But let the past go. We still look in vain in the Marxist
ranks for unequivocal condemnation of what is indefen-
sible on that side. Are there today any authoritative
Marxist sources which venture to voice a protest against
murder at the Berlin Wall? If we are to believe the party
position, that wall was constructed as a barrier against
the West. In practice, however, it has proved a barrier
against free movement in the East. Nor can it be said
of those who try to flee the East what you say of those
who seek to flee Cuba, that they seek only to preserve
their wealth and privileges; they are quite ready to accept
destitution and homelessness, if only they can be elsewhere.

Can you quote any Marxist sources, official or otherwise, that raise their voices in protest against the organized juvenile delinquency of Mao's Red Guard, or against
the barbarity of televising public executions in China?

Can one find a Marxist source that even ventures to question the Soviet Union's deliberate encouragement of Arab aspirations to annihilate Jews in the Middle East? I realize, of course, that the examples I cite can—and perhaps should—be explained as aberrations, not in the logic of Marxist desires to make of each man a creative center of initiative and responsibility—but an indispensable element of initiative and responsibility is the ability to engage in intelligent criticism and self-criticism. Would you say that the prosecution—better perhaps, persecution— of outspoken intellectuals in the Soviet Union or in the Ukraine and Poland constitutes open encouragement of criticism?

When we speak of criticism and self-criticism, I must, of course, express my reactions to your criticism of the Church. Here, I think, it is in order to begin at the end and work backwards.

It has been said, and with a great deal of truth, that, had the Church been true to its prophetic mission, and had it carried on the social revolution inaugurated by its founder, there would never have been any need of Marxism, nor would Marxism have caught on in a Europe which was properly oriented socially. With equal truth it can, I think, be admitted that for centuries the Church has implemented its consciousness of having an essential mission in the world by concentrating its efforts on preserving itself, and this even at the risk of betraying the profoundly social character of that mission. Although it cannot be said that the Church has not had the courage to oppose—even consistently oppose—those who had the power to destroy her, it is still true that in her history her predominant bias has been conservative rather than revolutionary. She has been slow to recognize the need of social revolution and has all too frequently condemned those who advocated it (although I should demand far more historical documentation than the nature of our discussion allows before I would accept your illustrations as examples of valid social revolution).

Thus, you are correct in saying that "fundamental Christian values" have been "obscured by a conservative policy in the Church." I will go further and agree that frequently these values can be found in a movement which is ostensibly opposed to Christianity—Marxism *can* help and perhaps *has* helped the Church to rediscover its prophetic mission.

When you demand, however, that the Church "give clearance" to socialism, you open the gate, it seems to me, to considerable confusion, precisely because of an unexpressed premise in your position. As I see it, for you "socialism" and "Marxist socialism" are synonymous, and I have serious doubts as to whether this identification is justified. This identification leads you to conclude, rather illegitimately, that any opposition to either the theory or the practice of Marxism is a refusal of the legitimate aspirations of social struggle or of revolution. Even granting that, in a confrontation of individualistic liberalism and socialism the choice must go to some form of socialism, or that private ownership of the means of production in its capitalist form is by no means a guarantee of man's freedom and significant productiveness, you are still taking a lyrical leap if you conclude that the only alternative is Marxist socialism. Admittedly, a reconciliation of the legitimate aims of socialism and of a Christianity conscious of its mission to promote the betterment of all men and of the whole man is "a consummation devoutly to be wished for." There is question, however, whether either Christianity or Marxism can accept a socialism which is based on a concept of man which it cannot accept. I can grant a Marxist the right to conceive of man in a naturalistic manner which is radically opposed to my conception; I cannot grant him the right to deny validity to a social order in which my conception of man is central. This is not the place, I suppose, to bring up again questions which I asked earlier, but until I know whether Marxism must look upon the religious conception of man as essentially a conception of "alienated" man, I cannot say that your form of socialism is acceptable to me or to any Christian.

As to your demand that the Church accept "the autonomy of human values" and "man's Promethean ambition to create continually both the world and himself," I have no difficulty in seconding it, provided that the hidden premise does not once more get in the way. To be "created in the image of God" is to be created a creator. To create, therefore, is the essential vocation of man; it is, if you will, man's share in "transcendence." Whether the Church has always promoted this creativity is, of course, open to question. I should venture to say, however, that history is more than a series of events in which the past imprints an indelible character on the present and the future. Thus, just as man has a history wherein, by his own creative activity, he becomes progressively conscious of what he is and can be in an open future, so too the Church has a history—too slowly moving perhaps—wherein she becomes progressively conscious of her commitment to man's creative advance. In all this there is no need to get rid of God in order to safeguard the "autonomy of human values" or "man's Promethean ambition"; if being created does not demean man, neither does participating in a creativity which is primordially God's.

There can be no question that "today workers are becoming more and more conscious that labor constitutes a part of the human person." By the same token, however, that is becoming more and more part of the Church's growing consciousness of its mission to modern man, which, as the Synod of Bishops in Rome recently emphasized, is no longer a commitment to the preservation of formal purity of doctrine. It may well be that this consciousness of a progressive role may lead the Church to "rejoice . . . to see humanity greet the appearance of another social system, less foreign to this morality" (of the Prophets and of the Gospel). Since, however, many churchmen were saying the same thing when that system took over in China, it is understandable that their enthusiasm should now be somewhat more cautious. In any event, it is not likely that they will see only *one* alternative to the oppressive capitalism which the bishops of the "third world" decry. The forward movement is truly irreversible, but there is more than one way of moving forward.

History bears eloquent witness to the almost inevitable divergence between theory and practice, and Marxism, where it has been concretely successful, is no exception to this. Granted that Communism has had great success where it has taken over in backward countries, has the reason for this success been the application of Marxist theory or the development of a state capitalism, which substitutes for a multitude of private employers one huge public employer called the state? I fear quite sincerely that the distinction between private and collective ownership of the means of production is for the individual largely a semantic one. Where it is still the small group which pays wages that control the lives and destinies of the people, it is not clear what it can mean to the individual to be *told* that all is owned in common. This, of course, may be only an aberration in the Marxist system, to be condemned merely as that, whereas capitalism should be condemned in principle as essentially evil, but it is difficult to see how you can demand such unambiguous clearsightedness in any but abstract thought with its untested a prioris. Quite frankly I fail to see that the establishment of collective ownership has in fact made it possible for all men under its dominion to "exercise initiative and responsibility in economic matters, in the production and distribution of the goods which condition the development of each and all." In the Soviet Union, for example, this universal initiative and responsibility is exercised at best vicariously. One need hold no brief for capitalism if one asks quite simply whether the sort of political power which collective ownership puts in the hands of a few is in fact concretely preferable. Do there even exist mechanisms whereby such a question of preference could be *honestly* put to the people? Nor is it to the point to cite vast improvements in terms of a rise in the standard of living among the underprivileged. Even granted that such a rise in living standard is a prerequisite to the unfolding of more "spiritual" capacities, such as initiative and creativity, you would be justifiably indignant with me if I were to point to the superior average living standard of the American worker as proof that capitalism is really the preferable system.

It is virtually axiomatic that "power corrupts," and, therefore, that you should—as do I—find much to be criticized in the power structure of the Church is understandable. At the same time, however, the unprejudiced observer cannot but be suspicious of much that emerges from the Communist power structure, even in its diverse manifestations. That the Twentieth Party Congress should have with one stroke erased thirty years of references to "the great Stalin" may or may not be understandable. That a large group of men, reputedly thinking independently, should arrive at such complete unanimity on all issues is scarcely credible—especially since that unanimity consisted in agreeing with Nikita Khrushchev! One does not, of course, expect truth in the official language of any political party, but it is distressing to find so much emphasis on the party—"our great, our dear party,"[2] with its implications that the good of the people is sought only to the extent that the party is the source of that good, that, in fact, the party is more important than the people.[3] So true is this that one suspects that such terms as "popular" and "democratic" have in the official language of the party only an a priori meaning—what the party wants is by definition "popular" and "democratic." Of course, the Congress recommends a policy of the outstretched hand to socialists who do not agree with the Communist process, but that is possible because "they err in good faith."[4] Is it at all possible to think or to say that the party errs—sometimes? Or would this be saying that the people err? Can only individuals make mistakes, which the party then corrects?[5]

The a priori has its negative side, too. If non-Communist countries unite for what they call "mutual defense," there is no need to examine into their concrete motives (erroneous as they *might* be); it is known without examination that their purpose is "aggression," just as it is known without question that an agreement among Communist countries is a "peace pact."[6] It is also convenient to know that, when socialist revolutions break out, they do so "by virtue of laws of historical development."[7] This provides an a priori answer to the complaint that Communist revolutions are exported as well as the assurance that a counterrevolution must of necessity be imported. This, of course, would be true, if it were also true that "only the working class, motive force of modern society, only the Communist Party, spokesman of its ideology, can have progressivist ideals."[8] I am afraid, however, that this is asking us to be too naïve.

It is interesting to note, incidentally, that any inclination to question the a priori can be discouraged by the fact that Marxism-Leninism has "science" on its side. "Our firm conviction that socialism will win in this great historical competition rests on the scientifically grounded awareness of the advantages possessed by a social system based on a collective ownership of the means of produc-

tion, a system which is a stranger to exploitation, to the inequality of races or classes, a system which is in a position
to give maximum satisfaction to the needs of the vast
laboring masses."[9] One shudders at the thought of
what might happen, if this turned out to be untrue;
science would no longer be trustworthy. This science, by
the way, even assures victory in war! "Our victories in the
Great Patriotic War were assured to a great extent by the
superiority of Soviet military science, invariably inspired
by the Marx-Leninist theory."[10] The trickle of aid from
capitalist countries was, I suppose, utterly insignificant!

Please excuse the seemingly polemical tone. My intention is not to defend the capitalist as opposed to the
Communist system. My problem rather is with the "scientific" character of the Communist system, and it does not
seem unreasonable to say that a minimum requirement
of the scientific is that it be truthful.

To get back to the question of religion—specifically to
that of Christianity—I quite agree with you not only that
what has frequently gone under the name of Christianity
has been an alienating force in man's history but also that
a large factor in the alienating process has been the emphasis put on "personal piety and the interior life of the
spirit" rather than on "the historical and social dimensions
of love." Here, however, I make the same appeal to you
that you make to the Church in regard to socialism: Condemn this, if you will but condemn it as a perversion of
Christianity. It is scarcely open to question that men
are sometimes asked to believe in a God who is unbe-
lievable. It is also true, however, that religion itself is
historical, that man's consciousness of God must be progressively purified, as man becomes progressively aware
of what his relationship to God must mean. This, I think,
is what is happening within Christianity, and the examples you cite on both the Catholic and the Protestant side
of what is gradually becoming more totally ecumenical

are proof of this. It may well be that the progress is so slow as to try the patience of outside observers, but I am not sure that rapidity is necessarily a criterion of the validity of a revolution. By the same token, we cannot say that revolution is the criterion of its own validity. There are revolutions which neither you nor I can recognize as valid, e.g. the one in Rhodesia. If, then, in the absence of an a priori standard for judging the validity of a revolution, Christianity is slower than you are in giving its stamp of approval, that should not be put down to an opposition in principle to all social revolution. The same can be said of its refusal to recognize that only the kind of revolution you advocate *can* be valid. What we all look for is the betterment of man, his free unfolding, to which revolution may well be a means—revolution can never be an end in itself, nor can its form be prescribed by an a priori theory.

With regard to revolution there is also a historical dimension to the problem which should not be overlooked. If we turn to the past we can, as you do, point to a number of abortive revolutions and conclude that they were abortive because of opposition from the incumbent power of the Church (thus, of course, ignoring that the most significant revolution of all, the Protestant Reformation, was successful). Might we not also legitimately judge that they were abortive because the time was not ripe for them, not merely because the thinking of the Church was not ready for them but because the thinking of man in general was not ready either? In the present, too, it is not always obvious that in a particular case revolution is better than nonrevolution, that the harm done by the violence of revolution does not in a particular instance and at a particular time outweigh the harm done by nonviolence. At least I see no a priori reason why the one violence is always to be preferred to the other. Nor need reservations such as these be construed as a denial of your contention that "the concrete struggle . . . against all that prevents millions of men from being men, creators in the image of God, can and should become the strongest link of solidarity between Christians and Marxists." One is not relinquishing this ideal, even as a goal of practical action, when one simply questions whether in a particular case the time is ripe for its effective implementation. One can, it seems, grant the validity of Marxist criticism of a situation without at the same time always granting the validity of its solution to the situation—nor need one's motives be impugned just because one does not see it as a solution.

There are times, of course, when the issue is too clear to allow of choice; one must take up arms against violence if one is not to be an accomplice in the violence. I might point out, however, that many whose motives are unassailable (except on a priori grounds) feel precisely that way about Communism. They may very well be wrong, but the evidence that they are is slow in coming through—and the evidence that points in the opposite direction is not repudiated by even those Marxists who do not have to fear for their lives if they do.

While we are on the question of Christianity and its attitude to social change, it might be well to touch on your interpretation of the traditional teaching regarding sin. Here I must rather blushingly admit that all too often the basic teaching that by sin man can hurt only himself and not God has been obscured by the juridical concept of sin as a violation of order. Even this latter, if construed as a violation of the over-all order of the relationships in which man stands to God, to his fellowman, and to his own destiny, would be all right. When, however, it becomes a violation of the arbitrary order established by human authority for the preservation of privilege, it is all wrong. There can be no question that a consistent conservative social attitude in the Church is intimately linked to this view of sin with its correlative legalism. The evidence that this attitude is changing—among the bishops gathered in synod at Rome—is too abundant to require verification. It is, however, going too far to say that, even in the past, the doctrine of sin was the "metaphysical expression of the social order which dominated the West from Constantine to the fifteenth century." (Nor does citing the highly controverted opinion of Burckhardt about the consciousness of medieval man help to keep things in perspective.) The fact is that there always has been a "curial" point of view which did not necessarily correspond with that of the "people of God." The latter, to be sure, suffered from this lack of correspondence, but the process of chipping away at the curial attitude has been unceasing and has made possible more than one successful revolution—the Marxist revolution among them.

At present the antilegalistic movement has reached such proportions that the whole matter of a canon law with its sanctions of sin is being called into question. This, of course, could mean greater liberty for individuals who look upon Marxist socialism as an answer to the aspirations of humanity, but it is not likely to constitute an endorsement of a system which has not yet manifested its ability to be rid of serious deficiencies. What is important is that the progressive mentality here in evidence can more readily see not only good but the hand of God in some of the results produced by a system which is professedly anti-God. Christians today are far more prepared than they formerly were to admit that God can reveal Himself in any movement which sincerely aims at the social betterment of man—even though they are still understandably suspicious of the movement as a whole, suspicious as to whether it concretely represents authentic progress.

The Church has traditionally held fast to the theological

axiom that "the sacraments are for the sake of man,"
meaning that man is more important than the sacraments
which serve him. In the light of a growing consciousness
that the Church as an organization is itself sacramental
in relation to the humanity it serves, we can look for a
growing realization that the task of the Church is not to
defend its own prerogatives but to defend man—remembering, however, that a necessary condition for its defense
of man may be the preservation of certain prerogatives,
e.g. its liberty.

In a somewhat roundabout way all this brings me to
what in my view is an unresolved paradox in what you
say regarding God and religion. When you speak of what
you expect, what you hope, of Christianity, you speak of
a "theology of earthly values," which, it seems, must
mean that the Christian's concern with God must become
less and less distinguishable from his concern with man
and man's creation of a better world. Not only do I share
such hopes and expectations, but I also see encouraging
signs that they will be fulfilled. On the other hand, however, you insist on a "radical discontinuity" between God
and man in regard to reasoning and system of values,
language and morality, which would seem to say that
concern with God and concern with man are radically
distinct, have nothing in common. You deny to religion
or to "the holy" a domain which can be separated off
from life or from solidarity with the world. Here again I
agree, but I cannot reconcile this with your insistence
that "only if God is truly God, the 'totally other,' strictly
transcendent . . . can man be fully man," with which I
could not disagree more thoroughly. For you "transcendence" can be an attribute of man only on condition
that it be not an attribute of God. But then you assign to
Him a transcendence which eliminates all significant
relation to man—in the interests of a history which is "a
creation, the total responsibility for which falls on man."

Once God has been thus separated from men, you say, He "can come toward man without limiting either his responsibility or his creative power." I can understand —even historically—your fear of a religion which is "opium"; I can even understand your fear that shifting responsibility for the course of the world to God will alienate man. I suspect, however, that, if you make this recommendation seriously, you can only with tongue in cheek assign to Christianity a role in your "brave new world." We simply do not believe in a God who can tell us nothing of human values, in a God who is unable to speak the language of reason, in a God who does not tell us constantly that we have a creative responsibility for our world and for the world of the future. What is more, we simply cannot see the assertion that such a God deprives man of autonomy as anything but arbitrary. We do not "place all authentic values beyond this world"; but we do say that a system of values which ignores God is a false one.

The question, then, which we both have to face is this: Can each of us continue to look upon the other's over-all value system as false and at the same time accept a common fund of values to which we can not only both subscribe but to the realization of which we can both devote all our energies? The answer to that question, it seems to me, depends on the extent to which we can look upon a value as to be realized, even though it is not adequately grounded.

At this point I should like to go back beyond your most recent remarks and return to what you have given in your books as your positive reasons for preferring the Marxist ideology to Christian faith in the struggle to bring about what we can call common goals. (I see no alternative, incidentally, to calling it an "ideology," no matter how firmly you insist that it is rooted in practice alone, since it does base practice itself on a conception of man and society which is ideal—even utopian.) In thus jumping back I shall, I am sure, fail to touch on some of your remarks which you consider important, just as you fail to touch on points which I consider important. This, however, is inevitable, if dialogue is to keep moving, and we can only hope that we shall have occasion later to take up once more topics which still need discussing.

Here, then, let me first of all make an admission: Although Christianity is essentially a revolutionary faith, historically speaking it has more often than not found itself on the side of reaction rather than revolution. The reasons for this have always been complex, and they have not always been good ones. Marxism, on the other hand, although I am convinced that it, too, is a revolutionary *faith*, is also a theory of revolutionary practice in the struggle against the very real injustices which the very structure of society embodies. It is my contention that Christianity is basically opposed to these very same injustices but that in far too many instances it has been ineffectual in opposing them, even though it has never relinquished Christ's ideal of love, without which opposition is not likely to be genuinely significant. This is partly because Christianity has often compromised with real evil in the misguided hope that it could thus protect a very real good, and it is partly because its revolutionary faith did not include revolutionary practice. Here, then, I can speak of two significant contributions which Marxism not only can make but already has made to the Christian struggle against injustice. However critical one might still want to be of Christianity, it is today far less tied to the folly of reaction than it was a hundred (or even fifty) years ago—and Marxism can rightfully claim some of the credit for that. What is more, today Christianity is far more aware of the concrete evils to be overcome and of the concrete means to overcome them than it has been in the past—I need but call in as a witness at this point

Pope Paul VI's recent encyclical *Populorum Progressio*.

Christianity, then, certainly can profit by serious reflection on Marx's thought, precisely in so far as it is a materialism, or, should I say, precisely as a materialism which is able to integrate the active function of human creativity. In the wake of Kant, Fichte, and Hegel, though not merely repeating them, Marx put strong emphasis on the subjective activity of man—in thought, in the creation of values, in the process which is history (i.e. man's transformation of the world and of himself by work). I wish, however, that you would explain what you mean in this context by saying that "practice [is] the *sole* criterion of truth."[11] It is difficult to see what this can mean, if at the same time you insist that this criterion must exclude arbitrariness. Even if you are unwilling to make the voice of reason the voice of God—a difficult enough thing to do—it seems to me that in some sense (at least logically) reason must precede practice, unless you want to identify reason and practice, which is at best arbitrary. What I fear is that your *"sens de l'histoire,"* which you say is not ideal, must, therefore, be real, which would seem to imply that the only direction history can take is the direction it does take—and this brings us back to the most undesirable interpretation of Hegel's "What is real is rational, and what is rational is real." I know you do not want this, but I, at least, do not see how you avoid it if "practice" is your only criterion. The difficulty is only compounded when you say that this practice (reason) reveals "objective laws of social development."[12] I can recognize without difficulty that Marxism has made invaluable contributions to our understanding of the genesis and structure of society (as have Hobbes, Locke, and Rousseau, but also Thomas Aquinas, Suarez, and Bellarmine), but I am still at a loss to understand what "laws" it has discovered and in what sense they are "objective." This you tell us in another place is the work of "scientific socialism," which has its "kernel of absolute truth,"[13] but that only deepens the mystification. Nor, despite its attractiveness, is the assertion that modern morality is the "invention of rules" of conduct[14] any less mystifying if it is to mean that practice—even if it is partially past practice—can alone give rules for practice (presumably "objective laws"). If, on the other hand, it simply means that no moral position can be so absolutized that it eliminates the possible validity of opposed positions, that is a sword which cuts both ways and has not, in the past at least, been too popular with Marxists.

In this connection, I realize, it would be naïve to think, as do some anti-Marxists (and some Marxists, too) that Marxism preaches a physical determinism in the "laws" of social development. The "laws" in question are seen as rational laws, whose determinism, as Kant saw so well, is in the ideal order, the order of reason. Kant, however, saw the need of seeking some criterion of rationality, even where the question was one of rational practice. Here I must admit that I too am struggling, but I cannot say that you provide me with any solution to my struggle. Your notion of the dialectic "as a constantly provisional balance sheet of rationality's victories for each great historical epoch"[15] throws a glimmer of light on what you mean by a solution, but it does not make sense out of the expression "practice is the sole criterion of truth." Rather it gives the impression that the dialectic, despite its realistic claims, is primarily a kind of logic governing thought about reality, whose only "law" is to be found in the assurance (somewhat arbitrary) that whatever inadequacies are to be discovered in former views of reality, it will be dialectic thinking which reveals and remedies them. This, in turn, means little more than to say that, if thinking is rational it is dialectical; which may be very profound, but practically speaking it solves little.

I am quite sure that you can define "practice" in such

a way that it includes a criterion for determining whether what is *de facto* done corresponds with what *should* be done, but it seems to me that you should say so more clearly. There may even be a sense in which what is done somehow reveals what should be done, but certainly it is not obvious. What, then, do you mean by "practice"?

Garaudy:

Your criticism of Marxism regarding its conception of practice as criterion of truth rests, I think, on a fundamental confusion. You constantly interpret the formula as though it implied a pragmatic conception of truth. Pragmatism is a conception of truth according to which that is true which is efficacious, which permits the conquest of nature or of man. This sort of pragmatism is, in fact, frequently characterized by a tendency to look for an immediate criterion of efficacy. Such a conception, it is true, leads to the foundation of a utilitarian morality in the narrowest sense of that term, i.e. from the individual point of view, an opportunistic conception, and from the social and political point of view, that of a politics of force.

Given the idea that what is successful is necessarily the good, it is understandable that out of it should develop a jungle morality which is expressed in the conditioning of the masses by advertising and, more significantly, in politically conditioning the masses to accept a politics of force. This makes it possible to camouflage under the guise of a crusade for freedom and a struggle against Communism a policy of hegemony aiming at world domination—from James Burnham's book, for example, to its factual realization in genocide in Vietnam. Proper to such a theoretical and practical pragmatism is to define the criterion of practice only in function of its immediate short-term efficacy. The Marxist conception of practice as a criterion is fundamentally different from and even opposed to this.

In the view of Marx and the Marxists, criticism based on practice is subordinated to a general conception regarding the meaning of man's life and of his history. The point of departure for all Marx's reflections on man is work. In some fine pages of *Capital* he defines what distinguishes work in its specifically human form from animal work, such as that of the bee or the ant. Characteristic of human work is its being preceded by a consciousness of its purpose, which becomes the law governing the movements which permit man to achieve it. With man and his history, then, there emerges a new dimension of becoming—the efficacy of the future in relation to the present. Thus begins a history specifically human in contrast to the purely biological evolution of animals. Man is not content to adapt himself to nature; he transforms it. What defines man essentially, then, is the power to create, a power to inaugurate a new future. At each stage of history it is this creation by work, this transformation of nature and through it the transformation of man, the constant creation of man by man, which basically distinguishes man from all the other species of animals. At each stage of history, no matter what the conditions of his work, of his creation, the major criterion which permits us to judge man or a human society is this: Does this or that action, method, or economic, social and political structure render it possible to make man, each man, into a man, that is to say a creator, a center of historical initiative and of responsibility on all levels—the economic, the political, the cultural?

Such a method permits us to base our political or moral judgment not on a utopia, on an ideal which would not have issued from reality itself, an ideal which would have no historical character but only the character of a revealed truth or of a truth called rational. This method permits us to avoid also a positivist conception, according to which one would be able to read in the real itself, as it is given, "laws of order." This method permits us to ground our political and moral judgment, at each moment of history, on a dialectic of the possible and the real.

At each moment of historical development, which is to say, at each stage of man's conquest based on his technical capacities to transform nature, a certain number of human possibilities are born. Let us take an actual example: Given the present state of development in communications, whether it be of men, products, or ideas, it has become technically possible to realize a planetary organization of the needs, resources, and hopes of men. Now, at the very moment when the present development of technology has made this human unity a technical possibility, our world remains a world torn apart. The ideal of human unity, then, is not in our time utopian; it is a real possible, and in our sense we have there a rule of conduct which permits us to orient all our thoughts and actions in function of this real possible and of its actualization. Thus, we have there the foundation of a morality and a politics which is neither utopian nor positivistic but grounded in this dialectic of the possible and the real and in the practical consequences which flow from it. There, I think, is the most profound definition of Marxist materialism and at the same time of the criterion of truth which it conceives as based on practice—historical practice.

It is in function of this criterion of practice that Marx, in *Capital*, institutes his critique of the capitalist system.

Beginning with the definition of work which I gave above, Marx shows what alienated work is: In every regime based on private ownership of the means of production human work is alienated, i.e. deprived of its specifically human character. (1) When the worker does not own his instruments of production, it is no longer he but his employer who fixes the goal of his work, thus depriving his work of its specifically human character. (2) It is no longer the worker but the owner who determines the means and methods of work even to the extent that the worker's movements are in some way mapped out and predetermined by the machine, and a man becomes a mere fleshly appendage of a steel machine. (3) Lastly, man is deprived of the product of his work, which becomes merchandise, something impersonal, which no longer bears the mark of properly human creation. Because man can no longer thus realize his humanity in his own work he becomes a double man. He tends no longer to realize his humanity in his work, his production, his creation, according to the very law of man, but rather in consumption. It is that, I think, which characterizes the consumer model of capitalist societies, particularly American society with all the alienations and all the forms of dehumanization it involves.

It suffices to recall these examples and the criteria of judgment employed by Marxists to bring out the radical difference between pragmatism and Marxism in their interpretation of practice as a criterion.

To say that the criterion of truth is practice means for a Marxist that we have every intention of elaborating a *critical conception* of truth. In contrast to dogmatic or idealist conceptions, Marxism shows that it is not enough to construct a system of concepts in order to attain truth —experimental verification is always necessary. Practice as the criterion, then, allows us at each moment to remind human thought of what is the very foundation of all critical philosophy: Whatever I can say of things—or of God—it is a man who says it. There is no criterion of truth internal to thought itself. From the point of view of the sciences there is no need to show that truth is essentially experimental. From the point of view of morality it seems to us equally evident that the only possible moral truth is the truth of our actions and not of our intentions. There again the criterion of practice makes it possible to avoid a certain hypocritical idealism by constantly recalling that a morality or a politics cannot be judged by what we say or think but only by what we do.

Such is the specifically Marxist conception of the criterion of practice, in contrast to a shortsighted pragmatism which does not order this criterion to a fundamental conception of man as creator and to a conception of man's history considered as continued by man. The ultimate question is not what means permit us to attain this or that proximate, immediate, and determined end, but what form of personal commitment, what form of economic, social, and political organization will permit us to assure to man and to each man the fullness of his human development, the access to creation.

IV   THE PROBLEM OF HISTORY

Lauer:

Although it is clearer to me now what you can mean by speaking of "practice" as a criterion of truth, there are still a number of points which have me confused. The first of these is a minor one and it concerns your reference to "pragmatism." If all this term refers to is a kind of utilitarian attitude which takes mere success as a short-term criterion for the validity of a course of action, I can see why you want to distinguish it sharply from Marxist theory. If, on the other hand, you are implying that what you describe corresponds in any way to philosophical pragmatism, represented chiefly by William James and John Dewey, you are simply the victim of a confusion which American readers will be quick to detect, thus missing perhaps what you really want to say about Marxism.

Another thing which confuses me, at least in the context, is your penchant for turning every criticism—or every question, since all I was asking for was an explanation of what you mean—into a denunciation of what the other fellow, particularly the American, does. You do not contribute to a better understanding of your theoretical statement about practice as *the* criterion of truth by showing what happens when the worker does not own the instruments of production unless you can show that the opposite actually happens when he does own these instruments. One might, of course, ask what it can possibly mean to say that the worker in a Communist factory does in fact own the machines with which he works. More significantly, however, I should like to take the three results of nonownership which you mention and ask how collective ownership effectively changes the situation of the worker. (1) Does the worker in a Communist factory in fact "fix the goal of his work"? If so, in what significant sense? (2) Does the same worker determine the means and methods of work in such a way that his movements are *not* predetermined by the machine which he tends? (3) In what sense does he own the product of his work, such that it is not impersonal? It is interesting to speculate on the "personal character" of the ball bearings—or even of the bicycles—which he makes. Are they personal in a way that capitalist ball bearings and bicycles are not? Since it is action which counts and not intention, I presume that it is the action of making them and not the intention he has in making them which constitutes the difference. Incidentally, the notion of "personalized" ball bearings is reminiscent of one of the worst features of American advertising.

One more difficulty before returning to the question of criterion. Although there has to be some sense in which it is true to say, as you do, that morality or politics are to be judged by what we do and not by what we think or say, there has to be another sense in which what we do is not the sole criterion for judging the truth of what we think or say. Just as it is quite possible to think or speak truly and to act falsely, so too the result of our actions can be good—or true—and the thought and language behind those actions can be false—and vice versa. Dialogue contains what you and I think and say—and we are both (as are all Marxists and all Christians) quite capable of being inconsistent with that in our actions, without thus providing a criterion of what we think and say.

There seems, in fact, to be considerable similarity between what you and the pragmatists mean by practice as the *sole* criterion of validity, and thus my difficulties with their theory continue to be my difficulties with yours. It seems to me, frankly, that you are saying that practice both is and is not the "sole criterion" of truth. I might point out, by the way, that in your exposition you nowhere even attempt to show that practice is the "sole" criterion of truth—only that it is an indispensable criterion for the judgment of what is to be done.

If you say that "practice as a criterion is subordinated to a general conception of the sense of man's life and of his history," you are, I submit, saying that practice is *not* the *sole* criterion. You can, of course, mean that this "general conception" to which practice is subordinated is itself a broader practical conception, arrived at through historical observation, but that should be made clear. More than that, however, it does not answer the question as to how you arrive at a criterion for true vs. false historical development. It is all very well to ask, "Does such and such an action, such and such a method or economic, social, and political structure, permit making man, each man, to be a man, i.e. on all levels a creator, a center of historical initiative and of responsibility?" But that in itself is a criterion of practice. I certainly have no objections, if you measure an abstract ideal against real, historical possibility, or even if you see the ideal as subject to real, historical growth. This permits judging the validity of a course of action by its practical consequences, but it does not eliminate the need for a criterion of the validity of those consequences. Perhaps the source of this criterion is "practical reason," but I do not see that as synonymous with "practice." In a genuinely pragmatic sense this can mean an "experimental verification" of concepts and theories, provided it is recognized that the contention that practice is the criterion of truth is itself a theory.

If we are to be genuinely historical we must, I agree, be able to measure abstract ideals against real, historical possibilities. Among other things, this will prevent us from looking back and criticizing failures to realize certain ideals at times when such realizations were not "real, historical possibilities." This is not the place, of course, to investigate each of the abortive social revolutions you cite against the background of such a criterion, but it does seem to me that the results of Communism have to be submitted to a critique based on the same criterion. We can well ask, "What is the form of personal commitment and what is the form of economic, social, and political organization, which permits us to assure to man and to each man the fullness of his human development, access to creation?" The point is that my answer to that question is not going to be the same as yours. It may well be that, measured against this criterion, a society in which the worker does not own the instruments of production has failed to realize man's dignity in work, production, and creation. It is not at all clear that, in a system where the state—controlled by the Communist party— owns these same instruments of production, the individual employee of the state is really better off in this regard. Here, too, theory must be measured against practice, and a balance sheet of *all* results must be drawn up—not merely a statement of obvious improvements in what was previously admittedly an extremely poor standard of living.

Garaudy:

You believe you see a contradiction between the contention that practice is the sole criterion of truth and what you call its subordination to another criterion, that of the sense of history.

I, for my part, believe that the "criterion of practice" manifests its full force and meaning only if it is defined not as man's immediate practice but as humanity's practice in the totality of its historical evolution. It is this which distinguishes Marxism fundamentally from vulgar pragmatism.

For a Marxist the whole of human history is a "practice": it began with the first action whereby man transformed nature, and, from the first chipped stone to the electronic computer this human practice has given to man new powers to transform nature and, by this transformation, to transform himself.

Each new power has opened to man new possibilities, and it is in function of such possibilities that, at each stage of history, a value judgment can be made regarding the real, based on a criterion which is not outside history itself. This criterion is, then, inseparably both practical and historical, since history itself is a practice, and, by the same token, practice is always historical.

Lauer:

We are, I think, getting somewhere on this question of "practice," but my difficulties are not yet resolved. To say that the "sense of man and of history" is not external to history itself may very well be true, but I fail to see that this judgment of which we are speaking is a purely historical one, even if one were to admit that only history reveals the elements which make judgment possible. We are, in fact, speaking of value judgment, and only if history itself is a value can practice be the criterion in question. To speak of value is to speak of what *should be,* not merely of what *is,* and I simply refuse to admit that history alone can in any intelligible sense provide the criterion for what should be. You might, of course, say with Marx that what should be is historical and what should not be is unhistorical, but that comes close to what we might call a private use of language.

That the criterion of what should or should not be cannot be derived from some sort of conceptual analysis, whether it be of human nature as a given or of some sort of divine plan which exists from the beginning and is presumably known to some favored few, I am prepared to admit. Thus I can see that the question, "What should be brought into existence?"—both as a question regarding the future and as a means of evaluating social, economic, and political structures of the past and of the present—is a perfectly legitimate question, the answer to which cannot be simply found in a given set of abstract principles. I can even go further and admit that the answer to that must evolve, keeping pace with the march of history and with the evolution of human structures. We can, for example, say that man should be free and that whatever promotes man's essential liberty should be brought into existence; whatever is an impediment to the flowering of that liberty not only should not come into existence but should be prevented from coming into existence.

This sort of thing might, for example, permit us to judge that on the large historical scale the advent of Napoleon was historically justified, whereas no historical scale can justify the advent of Hitler. The former, after all, was ultimately responsible for having broken with the feudal past and having ushered in the modern democratic spirit of the West, which is now spreading to the rest of the world, whereas the latter represented only a retrogression which can in no sense be historically validated. I might add, incidentally, that the application of such a criterion in retrospect, after the facts are in is a lot different from applying it to the question of what is to be done now with a view to the future.

I am not, in fact, convinced that the criterion works that neatly, even in retrospect, since Napoleon could just as well be credited with the universalization of a bourgeois culture which led Europe with the inevitability of fate to the collapse of that culture in World War I, but even that is not the point. I do think one can ask the question, "What should be brought into existence?"; and I do think that the answer to that question can both validly determine a future course of action and form the basis for a valid judgment of past courses of action. What I do not see, however, is that either the question itself provides a criterion for the validity of its answer or that history by itself provides the "objective laws" against which the answer to the question can be judged. Perhaps you want to say with Hegel that history is the steady march of humanity toward freedom (and rationality)—although I know you do not want to say that the plan of march was written before the march began. Perhaps you also want to say that only practice can reveal the direction the march must take at any given time, since the very meaning of freedom reveals itself only as it realizes itself—it is not revealed in an abstract analysis of man's nature. If that is what you want to say, I think I can agree with you and still ultimately disagree with you, because I do not think that the same statements have the same meaning against the background of two concepts of man which are diametrically opposed. When you and I say "man," we are both *referring* to the same being, but we do not *mean* the same thing.

Now, strangely enough, although we do not mean the same thing by "man," we can very well be saying the same things about him when we say that he "should be free," i.e. that he should be a "center of responsibility, initiative, and creativity." The difference, then, comes when you judge that a structure of society based on a naturalistic concept of man satisfies this exigency and when I judge that only a structure of society based on a supernaturalistic concept of man does. I submit, then, that in making these judgments neither of us is employing "practice" as the "sole criterion" for the validity of our judgments. Both of us are looking for a society which does justice to the reality of man; both of us recognize that the reality in question evolves with history; but I for one do not believe that history (or practice) alone dictates the direction that evolution should take.

Garaudy:

In a former statement I expressed myself as follows: "When we ask ourselves what we should do in order to do what is right, we are not seeking to conform to a pre-existing law as to an already 'given' being; we are asking what should be brought into existence but does not yet exist." This formula seems to you ambiguous and inadequate. You would like to know what *criterion* the Marxists have for choosing or determining "what should be brought into existence" as well as what should not be brought into existence.

There, I think, you are touching on the central problem of Marxism, what distinguishes it from previous philosophies and from "utopian" forms of socialism.

"The ideal," in whose name we Marxists propose to transform the real and to introduce new forms into men's lives, has not descended from heaven; it has not been revealed to us by some God, nor has it been taught to

102 A CHRISTIAN-COMMUNIST DIALOGUE

us by some tradition. It is not an exigency of an eternal "human nature," defined once and for all, or of a no less eternal "reason" hovering over men and their history.

For us the ideal is a moment of the real, not its contrary; and it is a moment of history.

That the ideal is a moment of the real Hegel brought out admirably in opposing the Kantian conception of the ideal. The ideal of today is the reality of tomorrow. For Hegel, however, at any given time the ideal is a moment of Absolute Spirit's progress. The Hegelian philosophy of history designates the victorious term of Absolute Spirit's story; it is freedom. With regard to this final term, the *Phenomenology of Spirit* emphasizes (as does the *Science of Logic*, by the way) that it was *already* present from the beginning. The result was that Hegel, who had the merit of having elaborated the panorama of a human history based on a rich store of empirical material, did not realize, once the whole structure had been assembled and he had determined the moments of the system's internal dialect, that he had simply abstracted from the totality of events a concept which permitted him to grasp the whole, a "provisional" concept, which is but a function of the totality of historical conditions. He did not consider, for example, that his conception of freedom as the final term is expressed in a form corresponding to the exigencies of the progressive bourgeoisie, which saw its "ideal" realized successively with the French Revolution, with Napoleon, and finally with a Prussia modernized under the reforms of Stein.

Hegel's *Philosophy of Right* shows the limitations of his concept of a "freedom" which would find expression only in the state, in the political sphere, whereas in "civil society," says Hegel—we might call it more simply, on the level of economics—the authority of the employer is in no way to be put in question. At the stage of bourgeois revolution—the French Revolution, for example,

or the slightly earlier American Declaration of Independence—"freedom" consists in giving citizens the vote,
thus enabling them in principle to share in government.
But this "democracy" stops at the gate of the factory
where employer monarchy begins. Such is the inequality
between political "democracy," granted in principle to
the "citizen," and the absence of economic democracy,
where a share in management is denied to the worker,
since that remains a privilege reserved to the owner of
the means of production, that political democracy itself
is vitiated. The first political constitution drawn up by
the first French Revolution, after a proclamation in its
preamble that "all men are born free and equal in their
rights," denied the vote to 80 percent of the French as
"passive citizens" because they had no property. The
principle was clearly affirmed—the one which Diderot,
too, had formulated in the *Encyclopedia,* in the article
on "Representatives"—that "only a property owner is a
citizen." The same thing had been true in what is called
the "Athenian Democracy" of the fifth century B.C.: 20,-
000 "free" citizens ruled over 400,000 slaves deprived of
all political rights.

It is worth noting that, in the name of "reason" and of
its flowering in "freedom," Hegel should in his *Philosophy
of Right* have succeeded in finding justifications for the
worst kinds of privilege, that of "entailments," for example. Such is the *historical* limitation of the Hegelian
principle, "What is rational is real, and what is real is
rational."

That is where Marx is radically different from Hegel.
As early as his *Critique of Hegel's Philosophy of Right,*
he broke down Hegel's great idealist *inversion:* Whereas
the concept had been derived from real experience,
Hegel made of real experience an unfolding of the concept.

In *The Jewish Question* Marx analyzed not only the

theoretical limits of the Hegelian conception but also the historical reasons for its limitation. This he did by showing—on the basis of a concrete example, that of the "freedom" defined in the French Revolution—that this concept does not express an eternal reality or an absolute ideal, valid always and everywhere; rather it expresses, at a determinate stage of historical development, the demands of a class, the bourgeoisie, thus revealing the limits of the concept's historical horizon. The insistence on political freedom, even given the limitations of its bourgeois form, constitutes great progress by comparison with the previous political system of feudalism and absolute monarchy. Still, a half-century later the "freedom," which had been a weapon directed against feudal reaction, became a weapon directed against the working class: After the revolution of 1830, it is in the name of "freedom" that legislation limiting the working day to twelve hours was voted down; such a law would violate the *freedom* of the employer! Obviously the working class has another conception of freedom, and for it socialism will be the demand to pass from abstract political freedom to concrete economic freedom, which means that the economy is not to be directed by a few owners of the means of production but by the totality of workers.

I have chosen the concrete example of freedom in order to bring out the *historical* character of the ideal in its relation to the real.

In speaking of "abstract freedom" I speak of that which in principle grants to each citizen a share in the political direction of the state but refuses to the worker any share in the economic direction of industry. Now, Marx did not see in the ideal of abstract freedom an expression of "Absolute Spirit" in its unfolding but rather an historical demand corresponding to the interests of a determinate class, a demand which in one period of history is

progressive, but which becomes inadequate and decep-
tive in a later period.

The criterion, then, has an historical character, which
we can thus formulate abstractly:

—from the theoretical point of view the ideal, at each
moment of history, is the rigorous determination of a
human possible based on contradiction present in the
real;

—from the practical point of view the ideal is the demand that this possible be actualized.

Let me illustrate this abstract formulation with an example. In *Capital* Marx considers socialism neither as a
moral demand (which would make it utopian) nor as
the automatic outcome of present reality (which would
reduce it to a positivistic and deterministic conception,
making its militant activity incomprehensible). Rather
he looks upon it as a method capable of overcoming capitalism's fundamental contradiction: The development
of productive forces, particulary of techniques, has resulted in gathering together enormous masses of workers
in large industries, thus increasing the possibilities of
production; whereas the relation of production, in particular the capitalist regime with its private ownership
of the means of production, has led to a paradox. Production has been socialized and is, thus, more and
more massive; but appropriation remains private, which
means that the owners of the means of production (of
factories, of the land, of huge blocks of stock, etc.) are
the privileged beneficiaries of this increase in productiv-
ity. The imbalance of socialized production and private
appropriation has led either to economic crises or to
wars which cause production to be oriented to other ends
than that of increased consumption by the masses—to
the destruction of the wealth produced.

For Marx, then, socialism is a method which makes it
possible to overcome this contradiction: It is an ideal born

at a moment in history, which will cease to be an ideal when it is realized and when man will be able to assign himself other tasks, the overcoming of other contradictions. It is in the name of this criterion that it should be "brought into existence."

We can consider a contrary example. Hitler's Nazism, with its ideology of racial superiority presented as an "ideal," went in a totally opposite direction. It was an ideal of Germany's worldwide hegemony, and within Germany it meant domination of the economy by a few gigantic industrial enterprises for whom racism constituted an ideology justifying their superiority. Such an "ideal" did not lead to a resolution of existing contradictions but to their aggravation by frightful destruction through war of the wealth created by men, by a destruction of men themselves and of their accumulated culture. There is an example of "possible" which should not be "brought into existence" but should, rather, be fought against with every possible force. On the basis of what criterion? Always the same one, a rigorous determination of what is a *human possible*. Now, from the time when men made their first flint tools to the discovery of atomic energy and the construction of electronic computers, at each stage the *human possible* has been man's capacity for a greater power over nature, over himself, and over his future. Whatever makes possible the augmentation of this power, i.e. what makes man more man, should be "brought into existence." Whatever leads to the destruction of this power by tearing humanity down should be fought.

There, I think, is an objective criterion which can serve as a common denominator for Christians as well as Marxists.

Lauer:

There need be no hesitation on my part in accepting your "common denominator" criterion for what man's activity should or should not bring into existence. If the "criterion of practice" means precisely that, there could, in fact, be no dispute on this point between Christian and Marxist. The criterion, however, seems to have changed somewhat in the course of the discussion. "Practice," it would seem, really means "good practice"; what good practice demands should be "brought into existence," and what should not be brought into existence is simply not demanded by "practice" at all, but by something to which we shall have to give another name. Still, we seem to be left with the task of deciding what is practice and what is not. It is that, you say, which contributes to the true advancement of man. To which I quite agree, but if practice is the criterion of truth, it is somewhat tautological to say that "true advancement of man" is the criterion of practice.

Somewhat the same could be said of the relation between the ideal and the real, or between the possible and the real. It is not without significance, I think, that, when you speak of a false "ideal," that of the Nazis, for example, you employ the term "ideology." This means, I take it, that a true ideal is one which should be realized and a false ideal one which should not. You are, of course, at liberty to call only the first of these the "ideal," and thus to say that it is related to the real as that which "should be brought into existence," but this does seem to leave the question of "criterion" up in the air. You say that your "ideal" has not "descended from heaven," that it has not been revealed by a God nor taught by a tradition, nor is it a demand of either eternal "human nature" or eternal "reason." I might point out that it is none of

these things for the Christian either; it is what demands
to be realized and is recognizable as such by human thinking (since it is going to require human action for its realization). Thus, up to this point you are not saying
anything that a Christian would not also say. If there is a
difference, then, it would seem to be in your implication
that only if one thinks along Marxist lines will one be
able to judge what is truly an ideal. The fact is, however, that one whose life and thinking are guided by the
ideal of love (which I find somewhat more concrete than
your "objective law") will judge quite as accurately as to
what should be realized, nor will he feel that his
"autonomy" has been compromised, because Christian
love has guided his thinking. To be quite frank, what the
Christian looks for (without denying a priori its possibility) is evidence that it is love which guides Marxist
thinking, too.

By the same token, the desire to avoid either some sort
of eternal "utopian" ideal or, on the other hand, a merely
positivistic criterion of fact, is laudable. Thus, the effort
to make the possible "historical" is not only understandable but genuinely significant. I, too, should like to
eliminate as a principle a somewhat common misinter-
pretation of Hegel's "What is real is rational, and what is
rational is real." If, however, you were to say, as it seems
you must, "What is historical is rational, and what is rational is historical," you could then accept Hegel's formula without difficulty. The only problem left would be
that of determining what is historical and what is unhistorical. The answer, I presume, would be: The historical
is that which resolves contradictions, and the unhistorical, that which does not resolve but merely com-
pounds them. Having said this we can, perhaps, once
more discern common ground beneath our feet. I am
afraid, however, that we can do this because we have
both slipped into our criterion something which is

more than "historical," at least in the ordinary sense of that term. If I say that not what happens is historical but only what happens as it should (anything else would be "unhistorical"), I have an impeccable criterion—provided I know what *should* happen and only if I do know this does the term "criterion" make any sense. If I go further and say that what should happen is that contradictions should be resolved in favor of man's advancement, I am saying, I fear, that contradictions should happen in order that they may be resolved—and I simply do not find myself constrained to accept that part of Marx's interpretation of history. Whether or not I can accept the Marxist *manner* of resolving contradictions (either in theory or in present practice) is another question.

Having come this far, however, I think we are now faced with another problem which inevitably flows from that of the criterion. We are still left with total disagreement in regard to our divergent conceptions of man. In terms, then, of a criterion on which we can in part agree, how are we to consider the question of personal responsibility, which must be also posed in terms of a conception of man in which we do not agree? I realize that one of the reasons why contemporary "humanism"—whether Marxist or non-Marxist—finds itself constrained to oppose religion, particularly the Christian religion, is its conviction that belief in God inhibits the autonomy of man, and in particular that it takes from man responsibility for the kind of world in which he lives. If it is always possible to appeal to the divine plan—not necessarily an exception in ecclesiastical documents—for the state in which man finds himself, one can well wonder whether Christian teaching is really concerned with man's responsibility not only for the world in which he lives but also for the improvement of that world such that it develops in a way which responds continuously to the developing needs of man. It is difficult to deny that Christianity at least seems to embody the sort of conservatism which reduces responsibility to that of preserving a set of values which is simply unaware of the future. Even the insistence on personal holiness or, worse still, on personal salvation, seems to be an abdication of responsibility for a better world here and now.

What I should like you to do, however, is what you have asked the Church to do with regard to socialism: Condemn the abuses but do not confuse them with Christian principle. As in any institution whose history is long, it becomes necessary from time to time to rediscover the principles which in truth guide it. Despite certain emphases, then, which a more than conservative hierarchy may place on given values which they do not question, there is an undeniable ferment in Christian thinking which constantly points to the emergence of new values in a world whose structures simply do not correspond to those of a morality which has been absolutized on the basis of abstract thinking. Among what we might call moral values—as opposed to the transcendent values which form the core of Christian faith—there is scarcely a one which is not today submitted to questioning scrutiny. This is not the place to discuss questions of personal morality, whose absolutes are no longer accepted even by Christians without question; they belong in a very real sense to an area of what can be called internal affairs. More importantly the values of traditional social structures are being called into question, and very frequently the answers which are being given even by clerics—in France, in Italy, in Spain and South America, even in the United States—are far from what a conservative hierarchy is capable of conceiving as possible. Christian theologians are ceasing to have difficulty in recognizing that changing structures of society call for changing structures of Christian response.

Thus, while recognizing that the popular picture of Christian commitment sees it as confined within a strait jacket of values which have been transmitted and accepted without question, I am convinced that not only the spirit of Jesus Christ himself but also growing Christian practice puts the responsibility for moral growth and moral decision squarely on the shoulders of the individual—provided, of course, that the individual is heir of a tradition and recipient of a moral training which does not permit decision to be the expression of mere whim. What I should like to be informed about at this point, however, is the status of individual responsibility in a Marxist framework.

One can, I suppose, make sense out of Engels' contention that in this framework it is no longer proper to speak of "good and bad," but only of "historical and unhistorical," provided the scale on which judgments of value are made is large enough. This raises, however, a number of questions regarding moral responsibility on the level of individual judgment and action. It is quite possible, for example, that the individual Christian may judge that the war in Vietnam is immoral (or, if you prefer, unhistorical) and may, therefore, refuse to take part in it and even demonstrate against it; just as it is hypothetically possible for the individual Marxist to judge that provocative action in the Middle East or in Africa or South America is immoral and to refuse, therefore, to support it (I question whether he could demonstrate against it). But it is also possible that the individual Christian or Marxist might not think that to cooperate in such actions is immoral. Presumably, he who sees events against the large historical background of what should or should not be "brought into existence" can judge that these individual decisions are correct or incorrect. The question remains: What is the responsibility of the individual, if his conscience still tells him something different, and who has the responsibility of correcting his conscience if it is erroneous? To this I might add another question as to how the individual, as individual, applies the criterion which permits him to distinguish the true from the erroneous.

This is obviously not the place to discuss the morality or immorality of possible attitudes in the examples I have cited. It does seem pertinent, however, to discuss the larger issue of individual responsibility. You know, I am sure, that in the mind of the non-Marxist man-in-the-street, Marxist collective conscience with its emphasis on "party character" (Lenin's *parteinost*) is incompatible with authentic individual responsibility, just as to the Marxist man-in-the-street religious authority is incompatible with individual moral liberty. Now, it is constant Christian teaching that the first principle of all human behavior is conscience, even though this *can* be erroneous. The individual has, it is true, the responsibility of forming his conscience accurately, and to aid him in this he has theological doctrine and a teaching authority. This latter should not preclude either the possibility of individual decision or the fact of developing values, nor does it deny that practical reason (perhaps "practice"?) has a very large role to play in the making of moral decisions. What the non-Marxist would like to know, then, is whether Marxism insists on the same degree of individual moral liberty and responsibility—and this in practice as well as theory. If the judgments to be made depend on the criterion of historical practice, to what extent is the individual capable of knowing how this criterion applies, when decisions are to be made? Or must he simply be content to agree that the party knows best? (The rather tardy condemnation of Stalinism continues to bother me.) I know, of course, that on the level of individual morality Marx was able to take over a good portion of traditional morality—since as a "superstruc-

ture" on a new "base" it had ceased to be "bourgeois"—
but I am still puzzled as to where that leaves the individual.

You might, of course, answer that Marxism is "the conscious grasp of the profound movement of our history"
and that, therefore, it contains within itself all that is
necessary for the making of moral decisions. The question remains, however, How is this to be made effective?
Does subscribing to Marxist theory automatically give one
this "conscious grasp"? Does Marxist "practice" guarantee
that Marxist action will be in the direction of this "profound movement of our history"? Do you in fact have
only Marxist principles to guide you in your own moral
decisions?

To be quite frank with you, I find something profoundly moving in a statement such as the one you make:
"When human planning is no longer at one and the same
time oriented and controlled by profit, inspired by the
interests of the few (owners of the means of production),
but by the real needs of all men, a great cultural and
moral change in humanity begins to be effective."[1] I have
no difficulty agreeing that the situation described in
these words is one which "should be brought into existence." What is more, I can recognize that in such a situation there could be effectuated a "universal conscious
grasp" which would orient even the individual conscience
in a way in which it is not now oriented. What I do not
see is that the words necessarily describe Marxism—or,
perhaps, describe Marxism alone. As I said before, if I
experience difficulties with Marxism, it is not with this
aspect of Marxism. More than that, in the practical order
I am convinced that the Marxist version of this ideal has
resulted in a situation where it is the few, the very few,
who decide what these "real needs" are, which are to
determine human planning. Nor do I have the kind

of evidence which would make me want to trust those few.

There are, I must confess, hopeful signs that what you are advocating is moving in a direction that could make trust more real. One of these signs is the very willingness to dialogue. If dialogue is to be real, however, it must be "dialectical," which is to say, it must be such that the opposing positions which confront each other are susceptible of change through the influence they exert on each other. Here, I think, I can appeal to something you have said—although the meaning I give it may not be exactly the meaning you intended. You say that moral values are to arise "out of the lived experience of contradiction."[2] The values, of course, are commanded by the resolution of the contradiction. You, I know, have in mind here the historical contradictions whose resolution ushers in a new structuring of society. I should like, however, to apply your criterion to the kind of contradiction which gives rise to our dialogue. Out of the "lived experience" of this sort of contradiction should come new values, but only if both positions are enriched (and thus changed) by the confrontation. The changes, to speak in a more Hegelian than Marxist way, will be implicit in the inner dynamism of that which changes, but they will be genuinely dialectical changes, only if the one position does not simply exclude the other. This brings me to the question of what changes you can foresee in Marxism, but that is a question we can leave until later.

Garaudy:

Your question, I think, is posed on two different levels. (1) First of all on the theoretical level: Does the Marxist conception of freedom and necessity, particularly in history, permit it to provide a foundation for personal responsibility? (2) On the political level you feel there is an incompatibility between the spirit of personal responsibility and party spirit.

Regarding the problem of philosophical foundations in Marxism for responsibility, the basic mistake to be avoided is that of making Marxism an "economic determinism." More than once Marx and Engels explicitly condemned such a caricature of their thought, insisting, as they did, particularly on the relative autonomy of superstructures (the state, ideologies, morality, the arts, etc.) in relation to the economic base and on the reverse action exercised by these superstructures (particularly by consciousness) on the economic base.

One cannot, then, reduce Marxism to some sort of economism which would be positivistic, mechanistic, and ultimately fatalistic, thus ignoring or underestimating the eminently active role of consciousness and responsibility.

Marx (and Lenin after him) constantly insisted that "it is men who make their own history," although they do not do so arbitrarily but under conditions always structured by the past. Thus, Marxism is essentially a world view which serves as ground for *a methodology of historical initiative*. Marxist morality, then, rests on this foundation: Man is fully responsible for his history. Let me quote what I have already written in *Marxisme du XX* siècle.*

> This morality which is history in the making, a properly human history whose scenario was not written by a God, by destiny, or by an abstract dialectic—whether of Hegel's Absolute Spirit or of 18th-century materialist "inevitable progress"—this morality is a continuous creation of man by man.
>
> At no point is this creation arbitrary, at no point is it determined. Man is at one and the same time totally responsible for becoming, not what he is but what he is not yet (nor is this inscribed anywhere) and obligatorily conscious of the historical conditions created by man's pre-

vious creations—conditions which obey necessary laws, to misunderstand or to despise which would lead to adventure and impotence.

Marx's essential discovery in morality came when he "defrosted" into human acts what had been crystalized into things and historical situations. This he did first by his non-Hegelian, non-Feuerbachian, but rather historical and militant conception of alienation, and then by the demonstration he gave in *Capital*, which manifests to man the possibility of the right to reappropriate his own destiny.

To demonstrate, as did Marx, how the activity of man as he creates himself in history is at one and the same time inseparably both necessary and free was to lay the theoretical foundations of all revolutionary activity and of all morality. In doing this he sacrificed neither objective necessity to personal responsibility nor the moment of subjectivity to the consciousness of rigorous laws of development.

In this Marxist view of man and his history the moral problem cannot be avoided: It cannot be replaced by the scientific and technical problem of truth, i.e. by the search for and discovery of a *true* order of things and of nature, which would give to moral conduct a foundation outside man. The study of social development's laws, even the possibility of sketching, at least essentially, the more or less probable path of a near or distant future, at no point dispenses us from taking cognizance of our own proper responsibility as acting *subjects* and creators of our own history and not *objects* of history so conceived as to reduce us to being only the result or the sum-total of the conditions of our existence.[3]

So much for the problem of a philosophical foundation in Marxism of personal responsibility.

You ask another question: Is personal responsibility compatible with the spirit and discipline of the party?

First of all, Father, permit me to find it strange and

paradoxical that the problem should be posed in this way by a Catholic priest, i.e. by a Christian belonging to a Church which has remained "monarchical" in its organization and "dogmatic" in its teaching to the point of never having abrogated—even in Vatican Council II—the alarming decision of Vatican I regarding the dogma of papal infallibility.

Even in the worst madness of the "cult of personality" and in the ideology of dogmatism Marxists never went that far.

I realize that today theologians and many educated Christians are deliberately skeptical regarding traditional dogmatism and affirm a certain liberty in regard to the hierarchy and its discipline. It remains true, nevertheless, that the fundamental teaching imparted to hundreds of thousands of Catholics continues to be the terribly dogmatic teaching of a "cathechism" and that, even for the best-educated priests, one of the most solemn vows pronounced when they enter a religious order, especially in yours, The Society of Jesus, is a vow of obedience. Was it not, incidentally, St. Ignatius Loyola, founder of the Jesuits, who said, "What appears to me evidently white I should believe black if my superiors have thus decided"?

I realize, of course, that today such precepts are no longer emphasized, but it is disturbing that they have never been explicitly denounced with the same vigor that we Communists have denounced the dogmatism and authoritarianism of Stalin. Believe me, if the General of the Jesuits or the Pope were to engage in such a public self-criticism, even several centuries after the death of the author of such a principle, I should be sure not to treat them as sarcastically as you do Thorez or Togliatti, who denounced and corrected the errors of Stalin as soon as they knew the consequences to which they led.

Without pursuing this polemic, however, I should like to go to the heart of your second question.

1) Party spirit is for us Communists a consequence of class spirit. The spirit of solidarity which an exploited class or an oppressed people requires as the most necessary form of responsibility sees to it that nothing—in our plans, our writings, or our actions—can be used by exploiters and oppressors to maintain or aggravate their exploitation and oppression. Let us consider some simple examples. When French colonialism was waging an unjust war in Vietnam and again in Algeria, the spirit of responsibility consisted first of all in denouncing and combating the fundamental crime. It was not to engage in some sort of "quixotism" or hypocritical individualism and thus "salve our conscience" or our "beautiful soul" by pinpointing this or that action of the Vietnamese or the Algerians—in themselves, perhaps, regrettable but in no way to be compared with the crime committed by the imperialist French. With regard to your own personal responsibility as an American citizen with regard to Vietnam or Latin America, for example, I let you be the sole judge as to whether your indignation against some shot fired at the "Berlin Wall" might be better directed against the sort of violence which amounts to genocide.

As I see it, the spirit of responsibility, for a Christian as well as for a Marxist, should begin there.

2) Just as *moral responsibility* is not to be confused with the subjectivism of an individualistic judgment, which would make us lose sight of the amplitude of both the problems and the crimes with which we are faced, so too *intellectual responsibility* in the search for truth cannot be proudly solitary. The present development of the sciences and of scientific research shows us that in all areas the work is teamwork, that the efficacy of each one's work depends to a great extent on coordinating the efforts of all. Does this methodic discipline and partici-

pation in common research in any way lessen personal
initiative or the personal responsibility of the researcher
who belongs to the group? Does the employment of a
common method, sanctioned by practice, lessen the schol-
ar's freedom of thought? or, on the contrary, does it provide him with the most favorable conditions for his full
development?

In my party something analogous takes place. For my
part I do not have the sort of intellectual vanity which
could claim to ignore the indispensable experience and
the indispensable practice of my fellow workers, whether
peasants or wage earners, who daily live the consequences
of capitalist exploitation. Now, what you somewhat ironically refer to as the "science" of the party comes from a
synthesis of the experience of thousands of men who are
faced in their daily life of work with this exploitation and
oppression. That is worth as much as a number of tech-
nocratic research institutes, without, by the way, denying the utility of such institutes or of the work performed
by sociologists and economists. Still, it would often be
worthwhile for these sociologists and economists to approach their problems by consulting the experience of
workers and not merely that of management.

Does this mean that the knowledge collectively elaborated by and in the party, based on the lived experience
of thousands of men, constitutes an irrefutable "absolute
knowledge" dispensing us from all personal reflection and
responsibility? Not at all. On the contrary, the party is
not some sort of abstract entity which transcends the
individuals who compose it. It lives and grows only
through the contribution of each member. Whenever this
is not the case, we are faced with a deformation of Marxism. Why identify Marxism with what is but a perversion
or a caricature of it?

The fact that we accept Marxism as a method of
analyzing theoretically the contradictions in reality and

as a practical method of resolving them in no way confers on us the privilege of an "infused science." Marxism is not a catechism of eternal and immutable "laws." I repeat once more, it is the constantly developing elaboration of a method for determining what *possibles* can grow out of the contradictions which are present and, consequently, a method which allows us to clarify our choice and direct our action.

This is not the place to show what grasp of reality this method affords us. But, since you often refer ironically to the "scientific" character of Marxism, I should like to remind you that this "science" has given at least this irrefutable proof: Thanks to it, in countries which are economically and technically a century behind others underdevelopment has been overcome—without any outside help—with a rate of economic growth which no capitalist country has experienced even in periods most favorable to its rise.

Finally, I should like to reply to your last question: Who decides what are the "real needs" of man? Here a comparison is necessary with what takes place under a capitalist regime. In America, for example, who decides what "real needs" are? No one. The very law of the system, which is exclusively the law of profit, leads to production for the sake of production, i.e. to a mechanical production, destructive of the human person and creating out of whole cloth needs which do not contribute to the development of man. The fine work of Galbraith on *The Affluent Society* and Vance Packard's writings on the art of waste have brought it out brilliantly. It is not an accident, then, that in the creation of "needs" the United States breaks the world's record in the production of L.S.D., whereas the Soviet Union is breaking the record in the construction of houses of culture and of recreational homes for the young.

Perhaps you could ask yourself what are the reasons

for this contrast, and then, instead of asking, Who decides?, you might arrive at a more modest conclusion. It is this: When the law of profit is no longer the law of social development, it becomes possible—even if the new system is full of imperfections—to found a human society which is no longer that of the jungle and of escape from the jungle. With all its imperfections socialism is up to the present the first and the only attempt to found social development not on the anarchical and inhuman automatism of profit but on the conscious activity of men.

Lauer:

Although it is not likely that anyone who knows the writings of Marx would accuse him of preaching "economic determinism," it is good for us to know that, in theory at least, present-day Marxism is equally vigorous in rejecting anything of the sort. It is clear enough, I think, that both Marx and Engels sought—as did Hegel —to reconcile the sort of necessity in process which is required for scientific theory and the sort of liberty in action which is indispensable for human dignity. Nor is it prejudicial to the latter to say that the present and the future are structured by the past.

The difficulty, however, is not totally dissipated, so long as it is still possible to speak of necessary "objective laws" of historical progress. The concept is understandable enough; it became current prior to Marx with the work of the British political economists who formulated such economic generalizations as the "law of supply and demand" or "Gresham's law" governing the flow of currency. The concept was taken up again by Kant and given a more rigorous philosophical foundation in the distinction he made between the freedom of the human will in initiating action and the determinism of the action once begun, since it is subject to the laws which govern actual events. Characteristic of laws such as these is that, although they begin as descriptions of what actually has taken place, they end as a priori prescriptions of what must take place, if anything is to take place at all.

Thus, whereas strict economic determinism is inevitably positivistic, mechanistic, and fatalistic, laws conceived in the latter way allow for a full measure of human historical initiative. Still, if they are to be laws and not merely factual descriptions they must be dictated by reason and they must bind a priori. This is simple enough, when what is in question is a physical law governing all bodies, even human bodies: If I jump from the roof, for example, I may be free in jumping, but my body is not free to go up rather than down. Such laws may also be applicable to large-scale human behavior, provided that scientific methodology can rigorously eliminate all contingent factors in its investigation. When the question becomes one of the individual's personal responsibility— that of being subject and creator rather than object of history—the matter is no longer quite so simple. Here it is that the contingent factors take on an importance that science cannot permit them to have. Your own example highlights precisely what I mean. There can be no question that in the community of scholars the initiative and responsibility of the individual are by no means compromised, because his research is bound in by the objective laws of the science within which he works. What is doubtful, however, is that the "objective laws of history," of which you speak, would not compromise the initiative and responsibility of the individual—or the group—which would "make history." I know, of course, that you can admit a plurality of forms of socialist revolution, but you would seem obliged to say that there is only one "law" of social revolution, and that it is Marxist science

which knows what this law is. In this I simply cannot follow you.

Nor is it really so paradoxical that precisely as a
Catholic priest, member of a "monarchical" Church, I
cannot follow you. This is really not the place to enter
into subtle discussions of "papal infallibility" or of ecclesiastical authority. I can say, however, that, were you
to believe honestly in a revelation, I should not find it
strange were you to look to some authoritative rule to
interpret that revelation. What I should find strange, however, would be giving to a "science" of history the kind of
infallibility which even a revelation or a dogma does not
have. I know, for example, of no dogmas regarding the
structure of society, the contradictions of history, or the
inevitability of class struggle. In my behavior it is still
conscience which provides the supreme rule—even though
I cannot conceive of that conscience functioning in a
vacuum. That conscience, incidentally, is supreme, even
where I pronounce a vow of obedience. What is more,
that vow of obedience is something which I take—quite
freely—and which I should not think of imposing on anyone else. I can think of nothing more vicious than a civil
society in which everyone was obliged to take such a vow.
I do not ask others to do what I do; I do not even ask
them to do what I say. This is the way I live out my own
religious commitment; it is not the way I articulate my
political convictions.

This, then, brings me to your remarks about "party
spirit." Although I can well understand the spirit of solidarity with an exploited class or an oppressed people, I
find it difficult to accept a political party as the self-
appointed locus of class consciousness. There is, of course,
a question as to just how democratic a political structure
can in practice be, and there obviously must be an organ-
ism which embodies the will of a people, even its somewhat unformulated will. That is what governments are

for. It is inconceivable, however, that the "objective laws" of historical development should have designated one party to perform this function. Moreover, here I think we must distinguish between the function that party in fact performs when it is not in power, as in France or Italy, and the one it performs when it is in power, as in the Soviet Union or China.

When you speak of exercising personal responsibility by expressing indignation over crimes against humanity— better still, by taking action against them—I am quite in agreement with you. I do not think, however, that a condemnation of what you call lesser crimes, especially when they seem to be part of a fixed policy and not merely a passionate response to frustrations, constitutes approval of the greater. Nor do I think that your indignation over the greater crimes absolves you from answering questions about criminal policies. One gets the impression that, having condemned Stalin for his unfaithfulness to Marxist ideology and not for his vast crimes against humanity, Communists are now free from the obligation of even answering questions about other crimes. I might remind you once again, incidentally, that I am not making any case for capitalism—above all, for its obvious excesses—I am trying to find out whether Communism is, in fact, better. It is somewhat ironic that you should speak of the brilliant criticism of America by such writers as Galbraith and Packard. I hope it will not be invidious to point out that, having made these criticisms for the whole world to read, Galbraith and Packard are still not in jail, which is more than can be said of critical intellectuals in the Soviet Union and in Poland.

What is perhaps more important than all this mutual recrimination, however, is that we get back to the Christian-Communist issue. We are both, I think, agreed that genuine social development cannot be founded on the mechanism of unlimited profits. But it should be clear to you as well as to me that, in criticizing any system for attempting to do just that, you are not criticizing them for being Christian. There has been little disagreement between us from the beginning regarding the over-all goals we should like to see realized. This means that while we can dispute the criterion whereby responsible human beings—whether as individuals or collectively— determine what should or should not be brought into existence, our agreement extends in large measure to a whole group of ends to be attained.

Still, we have been speaking of moral responsibility, and it does not seem to me that we can do so adequately if we speak only of ends. It is, I think, necessary to distinguish between the morality of the ends we propose to realize and that of the means we are willing to employ in realizing them. According to Christian teaching, if a course of action is to be judged good, the end for which it is instituted must be a good one. This is but another way of saying that the good we do may very well be vitiated by the purpose for which we do it. On the individual level this can be easily illustrated: If I give relief to a starving, poverty-stricken man for the purpose of binding him to me in such a way that he will help me to commit crime, the apparent generosity has been vitiated; it is actually evil. On the large scale the same thing can be illustrated: If an affluent nation relieves the distress of an underprivileged one for the purpose of ultimately exploiting the latter economically or of simply securing political advantage by expanding the former's sphere of influence, the help is no help; it is harm.

Conversely, however, the good end at which a course of action aims cannot validate evil means employed in attaining that end. Thus, nothing can validate the enslavement of either an individual or a population, even though the end in view is a sizable rise in a material standard of living. We cannot justifiably subject human beings to a totalitarian system, even though we be thoroughly convinced that only thus can they share the economic, cultural, and moral values at which we aim. There can, of course, be situations in which the greatness of an evil can in a very real sense justify what would otherwise be an evil in response to it. Frequently violence can be met only by violence, and a difficult judgment must be made regarding the sort of violence which can be employed in responding to violence. This sort of principle, however, is customarily employed by both sides in any conflict to justify the violence which each employs, and rational argument rarely succeeds in resolving the dilemma.

Now, there is another question hidden under all this, and it is that of justifying any and all means, provided they promote the end one is convinced is good. I am thinking here partly of the sort of tactic which Marx advocates in the *Communist Manifesto* or Lenin in *What Is To Be Done?* and partly of certain contemporary phenomena. According to Marx and Lenin, any movement which threatens the established order, no matter who initiates it or how unacceptable its principles may ultimately be, is to be supported because of the ultimate end in view. That is simply good revolutionary strategy. This carries over to the fomenting of unrest where it did not yet exist or contributing to the worsening of human conditions, both with a view to preparing the revolution. But there are other means which are used to consolidate the revolution which has already taken place, and one wonders how often they can be justified. I can see, for example, that it might be considered worthwhile to keep the population of East Germany steady, but I fail to see how that justifies shooting in cold blood those who seek to leave it. I can see how it might be deemed necessary to execute enemies of the regime in China, but I see no need of televising these executions for the rest of the people. I can see the possibility of convincing oneself (after the fact) that the Hungarian uprising of 1956 was not a popular one and contrary to the interests of the people, but I see no justification for the brutality of its suppression—by a foreign power.

What it all comes down to is just one question: Can you think of any means whatever which would surely promote the revolution, which would not be justified by that very fact? Presumably you are convinced that the best thing that could happen to France would be for it to become a Communist country. This means, I take it, that, if a majority of the French people does not want this, the party knows what the country's needs are better than the people does. Assuming for the moment that the party is right, there are a variety of means which it can use to bring the people around to its way of thinking. Since we are speaking of bringing into existence what should be brought into existence, are the most effective means by the very fact of their effectiveness morally acceptable? or is there a morality which can judge even the most effective means as morally unacceptable? Would terrorism, for example (which cares not who is hurt), be acceptable, so long as it can be judged the most effective means of persuasion? Would the long-term end in view legitimate means such as these?

I realize, of course, that there is an argument which says that force must be met with force or that the overcoming of a greater evil legitimates the employment of a lesser evil, but it is an argument which always serves both sides in any controversy, and I am quite convinced that it is rarely a good argument on either side. If, however, it is used on one side, it is not at all impossible that it is being used sincerely on the other. Perhaps there is need to put limits to the extent to which it can be used on either side.

V   POLITICAL QUESTIONS

Garaudy:

I like the way in which you present the theoretical aspects of the problem of means: We are, I see, in agreement regarding the fact that when "the established order" involves such injustices that millions of men are exploited, oppressed, mutilated, and humiliated by this "order," a revolution, even armed revolution, can be less costly and in the long run less "violent" than this "established disorder," which has become pure violence. Of this, incidentally, many Christians are today becoming conscious, including, for example, even priests and bishops in Latin America.

It cannot, then, be objected that the theological and moral obstacle to a dynamic and constructive reinterpretation of sin is the refusal of violence. For here again the view is given the lie by history, when we are no longer capable of seeing at what moment the maintaining of the established order constitutes a worse kind of violence than does a revolution against the same order.

Not to rise up in arms against Hitler's order was to

make oneself an accomplice in the worst sort of violence
—that of Auschwitz and Birkenau, of Lidice and Oradour.

Of what complicity in the physical and spiritual oppression of man was he not guilty who preached passivity
and "nonviolence" in the empire of the Czars, with its
millennia of repression, of illiteracy and pogroms? And
today, of what physical and spiritual oppression of man
is one not guilty who preaches passivity and "nonviolence"
in Latin America, where, as in colonial India, hundreds of
thousands of starving people from the Andes and the
region of the Amazon are collapsing along the roads?

We never have a choice between violence and nonviolence, only between two violences; and nothing can
take from us the concrete responsibility of determining
in each case where the violence is least and where it
contributes most to the free development of man. I repeat: To condemn the momentary violence of the slave
in revolt is to make oneself an accomplice in the permanent, tacit violence of the one who keeps him in chains.

We are not dealing here with a problem of "means"
but rather with a judgment concerning "ends," for, since
the time of Constantine, the Church has not recognized
conscientious objection. If, then, she can allow a Christian—even a priest—to bear arms and to take part in the
violence of national war, in the name of what principle
of "nonviolence" can they be forbidden to take part in a
social struggle or a revolution, unless what is condemned
is not *means* but *ends*.

We do not, then, disagree fundamentally regarding the
principle in question when we speak of the problem of
means. As has happened more than once in the course
of our discussion, our opposition is due less to the fact
that you are a Christian and that I am not than to the
fact that you are an American and—I hope you will

pardon me—a little too susceptible to a certain political propaganda, which you accept too uncritically.

I cannot, obviously, in a book devoted to the problems of dialogue between Christians and Marxists, take up one by one all the political problems which you raise, and even less can I give to each an exhaustive answer. I shall, then, limit myself to a few remarks on the way you approach the problems.

When, for example, you bring up more than once the German problem, you are satisfied to use the expression "the Berlin Wall" and to refer to the incidents which have taken place there, taking as the basis for your remarks one-sided information and a narrow problematic. If one wanted to approach the German problem seriously it would be necessary to begin by considering this question which is crucial for the future of Europe and of peace: In which section of Germany is the danger of Hitlerism in the process of being reborn; where are the former Nazis reorganizing to take up once more their adventure which was interrupted by the defeat of Hitler? Then it would be necessary to ask oneself this second question: Who is it that tolerates and encourages this rebirth of the spirit of revenge, since all the key sectors of German industry are controlled by American capital? When the problem is put in this perspective, each particular fact (including the "Wall") is situated in its context and takes on a new meaning, especially for Europeans who have known, as I have, concentration camps and the crimes of German militarism.

I shall not reply to the question about Chinese television, which I have never seen—nor have you—an area where we run a strong risk of discussing facts which are in no way established. But there, too, since I devoted to this question an entire book, *Le problème chinois,* in which I am very critical in regard to Mao and his "Red Guard," may I say that "facts" such as those you have cited, even if they are not created out of whole cloth by certain propaganda offices (neither of us knows), should also be situated against the background of a century of crimes committed against China, from the Opium War to the exactions of Chiang Kai-shek. They should also be seen against the background of a revolution which puts before the world in a tragic manner the problem of the world's future, the problem of models of civilization and of the very ends of society.

As for Hungary, there too you put the question in a very one-sided way. Like everyone else, you deplore the necessity of armed conflict there, but you ignore or forget that, if the insurgents had 4000 victims, in the bloody terror they had instigated the week before they massacred 10,000 persons, that they announced their intention of taking back from the peasant workers their lands in order to give them back to the former feudal landed proprietors, that they resurrected such a violent antisemitism that Jewish organizations in Hungary sent to Israel a desperate appeal to evacuate 200,000 Jews whose lives were menaced. You forget that Horthy, Hungary's former fascist dictator, from Portugal welcomed with joy this counterrevolution and that, harsh as the necessity may have been, Soviet intervention prevented the reconstitution of a Nazi stronghold in the heart of Europe.

The fact that it was incontestably mistakes made previously by Hungarian Communist leaders which thus permitted fascist forces to exploit popular dissatisfaction and to reintroduce refugees in large numbers in order to rebuild their fascist militias, does not change the fundamental problem. Granted that mistakes had been made, bringing with them dramatic consequences, should a nucleus of Hitlerism, that of the "pointed crosses" and of Horthy, have been allowed to revive in the heart of Europe?

Once we get beyond the realm of principles the problem of means, on the historical level of facts, can be discussed seriously only on the basis of objective and complete information and in an analysis where each fact is placed in the over-all situation which gives it its sense.

Lauer:

Although I should like to be able to decry violence in any form, on any side of a dispute, there seems little question that you are right in saying that in any concrete situation we must ask, on which side is the violence greater, on which side is it more criminal. When we do, I agree, we shall frequently have to say that the violence which perpetuates oppression is worse than that which seeks to overcome it. If indeed it is true that we are not faced with a choice between violence and nonviolence but only between two violences, then in the abstract the choice is clear. In concrete situations, however, questions can still be asked; not, perhaps, whether violence as such may be justified, but whether this violence in these circumstances is a legitimate means. Of this nature were the questions I asked.

Thus, I have no intention of bringing up the "German problem," which is obviously too complex for treatment in a discussion such as ours. The point is that to bring up the question of the "Berlin Wall" is not to bring up the whole of the "German problem." Nor do I think that I base myself on one-sided information when I bring up the question. Granted that we are both guided by certain predispositions in the interpretation of facts—as when you see a major recrudescence of Nazism in the most unfortunate aberrations of a small number of West German extremists—still facts remain facts, and the facts of the Berlin Wall are there for all the world to see. There are worse facts, no doubt, but that is no excuse.

As for Chinese television, you are quite correct in saying that neither of us has seen it. Perhaps my information was inaccurate (it was not, by the way, secured from American newspapers). That we can let go. I cannot, however, let go your interpretation of the Hungarian insurrection of 1956, wherein statements of fact and statements of value are mingled somewhat alarmingly. You say, for example, that the insurgents lost 4000 whereas the other side lost 10,000. It would be interesting to know the source of your figures, since not even the thoroughly untrustworthy Kadar regime's Hungarian White Book (*The Counter-Revolutionary Forces in the October Events in Hungary*) contains anything like them. There is much literature, scholarship, and documentary proof connected with the Hungarian uprising. We can find on record every newspaper reference, every handbill, and each word transmitted by every radio station. There is nothing that indicates that the Freedom Fighters "massacred 10,000 persons," while there is ample evidence that the AVD did massacre thousands and that about 2000 executions were carried out after November 4, 1956. I might also mention that all this took place long after the Twentieth Party Congress had denounced Stalinism.

You go on to say that "they announced their intention of taking back from the peasant workers their lands in order to give them back to the former feudal landed proprietors." As a matter of fact "they" did not. There is no evidence whatever to support your claim. Perhaps Cardinal Mindszenty did in one radio broadcast, but he was repudiated by the insurgents, the majority of whom were workers and students. You say that the lives of 200,000 Jews in Hungary were menaced. Since at the time of the uprising there were approximately 120,000 Jews in Hungary, many of whom were among the leaders of the revolt and among the young freedom fighters, your figures obviously demand careful scrutiny.

At the time of the Hungarian uprising all radio broadcasts could be monitored from outside Hungary. From the demands made on these broadcasts it was quite clear that the uprising was not a counterrevolution—it was not even anti-Communist—it was fighting for a freedom which the people had lost; all their demands were compatible with the principles of a modern socialist state. Since U.N. observers were not permitted inside Hungary, their report which stated that it was a spontaneous national uprising without outside assistance may have been inaccurate, but I have yet to see the objective evidence supporting the opposite contention. Would you in all honesty want all the evidence aired once more, or would it not be more prudent to join eminent Marxist thinkers who feel that this was a vast mistake which Communism can only continue to regret? I, for my part, would prefer simply to take the words of Albert Camus, who wrote on September 1, 1957: "The subjugated and enslaved Hungary did more for the cause of freedom than any other people in the world during the last twenty years." It may seem that I am putting somewhat disproportionate emphasis on your report of the Hungarian uprising, but since you are the one who demand that serious discussion be based on "objective and complete information," it does seem necessary to assure you that you do not have a monopoly on that.

Now, although I am inclined to think that the relation of means to ends in this and other examples belongs somehow to the very logic of Communist revolution (and your need to defend the suppression of Hungarians tends to confirm my suspicion), I am prepared to treat such concrete examples as aberrations from a purified Marxism. I cannot but condemn the aberrations, just as I condemn aberrations from Christian principle. I think, however, that we can now look at the question of means from a different point of view, which touches more closely the larger question of the end upon which we both agree, i.e. the advancement of man, the realization of his potentiality to be a center of initiative, creativity, and responsibility. With regard to this we can ask whether Marxism or Christianity can contribute more to the realization of this goal.

Here, however, I must say that the very asking of this question initially puts me in a disadvantageous position. Christianity is a religion, the form of expressing a faith, which, although it is essentially a commitment to both God and man, a manner of taking one's place in the world, is not, as such, directly a *program* for economic, social, or political action aimed at bringing about a desired state of affairs. It cannot, therefore, be judged as a program would be judged. It is not committed to any particular economic, social, or political system, precisely because it is open to the changing structures of man's social evolution, and yet it is incompatible with such political systems as Nazism, Fascism, or totalitarianism in any form, precisely because it cannot accept any political structure which would lay claim to the totality of man's loyalties. It is committed to man, to all men, to the future of man—here on earth as well as hereafter—and it must encourage and support whatever movement it is convinced will best promote the betterment of man.

What the betterment of man will mean, however, Christianity does not find in "objective laws" of historical development, since it can find no justification for calling them "laws." Rather, it finds the meaning of man in his encounter with Christ, who is the revelation of what it is to be man. Still, this encounter and revelation does not preclude the progressive realization of what it is to be man, and so Christianity is not bound to a static, nonhistorical view of man. Precisely because Christianity has been around a long time and has learned to live with the weakness of man, it can take as both its guiding principle and its final aim a love which will be truly a love of each for all and of all for all, without succumbing to the utopian dream of a political system which will make of love the "objective law" of human relations. Nevertheless, because it is a religion of love, Christianity should be able to integrate into its horizon of values the legitimate ideals and aspirations of those who also seek the betterment of man. At the same time it reserves to itself the right to judge the legitimacy of the means which are proposed for the attainment of that end.

All this is very abstract, I know, and Christianity—or at least its official representatives—has more than once judged too harshly not only the means but also the ideals and aspirations of those who sought social change. Fortunately, the individual Christian has no obligation not to be severely critical of what he considers backwardness in this regard. The point is that being severely critical is not being destructive; the Christian is sincerely convinced that the answer to man's problems, although not already inscribed in an eternal model, are, nevertheless, progressively emerging in an ongoing Christian commitment. We may not have a solution to these problems, because all the solutions we have seen are to us unrealistic and doctrinaire, but we do have a concept of man which makes any naturalistic interpretation seem truncated and unrealistic. Marx himself had a horror of utopian socialism, because it was based on an abstract conception of man which had no link with concrete history. We have a horror of Marxist socialism, because it pretends to be based on a historical concept of man but is in fact based on a naturalistic prejudice which can be supported only by a faith which is for the most part negative. Marxism pretends to be scientific, but it is so only by its opposition to a concept of man which does not even pretend to be scientific. Perhaps you can show me the probative value of Marxist "science," but I'm afraid it will persuade no one but no-longer-existent German philosophers of nature.

On the other hand, there is no doubt that the argument of history does not speak well in our favor—especially if you insist on identifying Christianity with official Catholic hierarchical positions. Since I have already spoken to that question, all that remains, it seems, is to ask whether this criticism of Christianity-at-its-worst versus Marxism-at-its-worst is really serving any purpose.

Garaudy:

Before going to the heart of your question, permit me to refer back to an expression you used, which is historically inaccurate: Marx did not at all have a "horror" of utopian socialism. In fact, more than once he spoke with high praise of Fourier, Saint-Simon, Theodore Dézanny, and even of Thomas Münzer. He viewed with respect and admiration this sort of human protest against the contradictions of a society and this sort of dream of a more human society. Marx judged the utopians historically; he could not blame them for not elaborating a concrete and practically realizable conception at a time when the historical conditions for this realization did not exist.

Thus, he praises certain intuitions of theirs, like those of Fourier and Saint-Simon regarding the anarchy of capitalist production, the role of the state, the education of the future, and regarding Communism itself. At the same time, however, he shows the limits of their thought, which are the limits of their times. He shows especially how important were the means of realization they proposed at a time when the laboring class was not yet an independent historical force.

I should hope, then, that you would have no more "horror" of Marxist socialism than Marx had of the utopians; all the more since the reasons you invoke are hardly convincing because they do not correspond to reality. It is absolutely contrary to the thought of Marx to base it on a "naturalistic" conception of man, and worse still to compare him with the "philosophers of nature." His critique of Schelling's philosophy of nature or of the "naturalism" preached by the French philosophers of the eighteenth century on the one hand, and on the other, his critique of Feuerbach permit no doubt on the subject. Marx's concept of man is essentially historical, and his critique of Bentham in *Capital* emphasizes once more the difference between the process of nature and the history of man. Marx establishes this difference in *Capital*, where he refers to Vico: Man makes his own history. As early as the Manuscripts of 1844 the break with the "naturalism" of earlier materialists was complete, since at that early stage his conception was of man's continuous self-creation, harking back to Fichte, the very antipodes to naturalism.

There you have a question of fact; it suffices to look at the texts.

Now to the basic question, where once more you speak ironically of Marxism's "scientific" possibilities and of its efficacy in what concerns the advancement of man.

The criterion of practice, understood in the Marxist sense which I have already defined, permits me to reply directly to the question as to who best realized the advancement of man.

First of all, here the most elementary objectivity demands that we neither compare Christianity as it should be with Marxism as it is, nor Marxism as it should be with Christianity as it is. We must compare point for point what is comparable. Thus, we must begin by comparing Christianity as it is with Marxism as it is, i.e. the two doctrines as they have been historically realized.

From this point of view I find it necessary to say to Christians that, in the area of historical realization, it would be well for them to approach their own teaching with considerable modesty. To me it seems difficult in the light of Christianity's historical, social and political realizations over the course of twenty centuries, that Christians should today make any claim to give lessons to others.

Whatever may have been the initial beauty and grandeur of the Christian message, historically speaking it remains true that, despite isolated preaching, a number of martyrs who are to be admired, and a conception of man which we continue to praise, the Church as an institution has constantly played the fundamentally negative role of justifying the established disorder; in particular it has sanctioned all forms of class domination. Successively it has, from a doctrinal point of view, legitimated slavery, serfdom, and finally the wage system in the capitalist world. It has constantly condemned all movements which have tried to put an end to these forms of human servitude, from the revolt of the circumcellions, against whom St. Augustine himself did not hesitate to call upon the secular arm, to the rebellion of the German peasants under Thomas Münzer at the time of the Reformation, when even Luther called upon the princes to repress them. The same was true of the French Revolution, whose very principles were condemned; and it took two centuries before a pope was to recognize that these principles were in conformity with the fundamental inspiration of Christianity. It was true, finally, in the systematic condemnation of all the workers' revolutions of the nineteenth century—the repression of the Commune sanctified and justified by the support of the Church and ultimately the condemnation of all socialist revolutions.

As Father José Gomez Caffarena wrote in the Spanish Jesuit review, *Razon y Fe,* for December 1964: "Through a sad paradox, Christianity, the religion of love, has historically served as a cover for the worst sorts of self-ishness."

As for socialism, no matter what may have been its aberrations—even bloody ones—in the course of which it was to be built up in perennially underdeveloped countries, no one can ignore its historical efficacy, not only in its capacity to overcome underdevelopment with minimum delay but also from a specifically human point of view.

It is a fact that during the ten years of Batista's dictatorship in Cuba—under American protection—illiteracy did not decrease by 1 percent, whereas in three years under a socialist regime it has been practically eliminated. One could say the same sort of thing with regard to prostitution. This is true of all socialist countries, and perhaps it is one of the things that led a theologian like Harvey Cox of Harvard to recall that in the Biblical tradition it happens that Jahweh turned to unbelievers like Cyrus, King of the Persians, for the accomplishment of this work. The work of God in our age, writes Cox,[1] may today be accomplished by men who are no longer Jews or Christians—as Cyrus was not—and who today might be called Kosygin or Fidel Castro.

Here the discussion of who best realized the advancement of man is no longer a theological or philosophical one. I think that the essential problem to be resolved is a problem of information. If we have the same criteria of man's advancement—to make of each man a man, i.e. a creator—the reply to the question as to who best realizes this advancement becomes a technical one. It is a question of judging on the basis of objective information the struggle to overcome underdevelopment and to create new social relationships, taking into account historical burdens and numerous setbacks, for example, in the building of socialism. It is a question of examining in each case what are the economic structures and political institutions which permit man to reach effectively his true human condition.

Lauer:

When it comes to a dispute over individual words, sometimes the best thing to do is simply drop the word, especially if it is of no importance. I have no objections, for example, to accepting your contention that Marx did not have a "horror" of utopian socialism, knowing that even in the *Manifesto* he had some kind words to say about utopians in the past. The word is utterly unimportant; the fact is that in the same *Manifesto* he vigorously opposes contemporary utopian socialism precisely as an obstacle to social progress, and this because it seeks to reconcile rather than exacerbate class antagonisms. It is nonrevolutionary and, *therefore,* invalid (antihistorical) socialism.

> Therefore, although the originators of these systems were, in many respects, revolutionary, their disciples have, in every case, formed mere reactionary sects. They hold fast by the original views of their masters, in opposition to the progressive historical development of the proletariat. They therefore endeavor, and that consistently, to deaden the class struggle and to reconcile the class antagonisms. . . . By degrees they sink into the category of the reactionary conservative socialists depicted above, differing from these only by more systematic pedantry, and by their fanatical and superstitious belief in the miraculous effects of their social science.[2]

As a matter of fact, then, I do not have more "horror" of Marxist socialism than Marx had of the utopians. As you already know, I see too much good not only in the ideal of human advancement through human activity but even in the revolutionary character of the change that must take place, for me to oppose the *ideal* intransigently. My problem is not socialism; it is the kind of Communistic socialism which Marxism advocates—and even there I am trying to find out if it is susceptible to the kind of historical development which would make it more acceptable.

That brings me to another word you do not like, i.e. "naturalism." Here, I am afraid, I cannot very well drop the term without failing to say what I want to say. To avoid confusion, however, I can assure you that there is nothing further from my mind than to assert that Marx was "naturalist" in the way you say he was not. There we have an example of the kind of confusion which arises from the fact that we speak two different philosophical languages. It simply did not occur to me that, speaking in the twentieth century, I could be interpreted as referring to the "naturalism" of eighteenth-century French philosophers—nor did I anywhere compare Marx with Schellingesque "philosophers of nature." There can be no question that Marx's concept of man—like Hegel's—is essentially historical and in that sense not "natural." What I think of—what any modern American would think of—when I say "naturalism" is the sort of thing that Engels speaks of (I am sure Marx would not disagree) when he says, "Nothing exists outside of nature and man."[3] If you do not want to call that "naturalism," that is perfectly all right with me, but I still want to register my opposition to the "transcendent" which does not transcend, to the "objective historical laws" to which man is subject and which are established in a "dialectic of nature," in short to the "naturalism" which, although it may not be "mechanistic," is still essentially "atheistic." It is not a question of being ironical when speaking of Marxist "science"; rather it is a conviction both that science does not have (nor can it arrive at) all the answers in regard to man and that the answers which Marxism does have—even the ones I agree with—are not all "scientific." That I consider to be to Marx's credit!

As for the fact that the Church, after its revolutionary beginnings, became progressively more unwieldy, slow moving, and hence frequently "unhistorical" in its sanctions and condemnations, I have no hesitation in admitting that a historical examination of conscience can be embarrassing. Once again, however, you simply indicate the advantage of having a short history rather than a long one. Nor, in your list of accusations do you always take account of the fact that a condemnation may be directed not at the affirmation of truth but at the denial which is inseparable from it. It is unquestionably a "sad paradox" that the religion of love should have been misused as a cover-up for selfishness. What is clear, I think, is precisely that this is a "misuse" of Christianity. I should be happy to grant that the examples I cited are also aberrations and not proper to the logic of Marxism—if only you would also admit the same, rather than simply attack what I do not defend!

To say what capitalism does not do is not to say what Communism does—but more importantly, it is not to say anything about what Christianity does or does not do. There is, however, another problem here. Strictly speaking, when we ask the question, Who best realizes the advancement of man?, we cannot ask it in the same way in regard to Marxism, which is a program of practical action, and Christianity, which is a religious commitment—to man as well as to God. If Christianity is to have a program of practical action in the modern world, it may well have to borrow one—and it might even borrow it from Marxism, if it can be shown that that does not involve an insoluble contradiction; one of the things we are trying to find out.

If it is without purpose to speak of the Christian religion in terms of a program of political action for the realization of human goals, it is certainly not without purpose to speak of Christian concern for social reform or of a developing Christian teaching in this regard. In order to do this, however, I must focus my remarks in a way which up to this point I have been trying to avoid. I must speak of what we might call the official position of the Roman Catholic Church on social matters. This I do for two reasons: It is the only position with which I am sufficiently familiar to speak at all; it is the only position I know of which has the authority to commit a major segment of the Christian world.

What I should like to stress here is that it is a teaching still in the process of developing, which means that, even though one can legitimately find fault with its inadequacies along the way and even ask why it so often lags behind concrete social development, it is nevertheless moving in the direction of taking profound account of humanity's social aspirations.

Thus, although it is easy to point out inadequacies in the social teaching of Pope Leo XIII in his encyclical *Rerum Novarum,* written in 1891, it is still necessary to recognize that, against the background of traditional ecclesiastical conservatism, it was in its day a revolutionary document (literally translated, its title means "Of Revolution"). It is not without significance, I think, that Leo XIII was accused by ultraconservative Christians of "preaching Communism"! It was a beginning of official insistence that "Christian charity" can never be a substitute for human justice, that laborers and the poor had *rights* which could never be satisfied by a mere generosity which did not recognize them as rights.

That Christians—particularly Christian industrialists—were slow to implement the demands of Leo XIII is attested to by the fact that forty years later Pius XI found it necessary to write *Quadragesimo Anno* as a direct sequel to the earlier encyclical. Although Pius XI did cite certain improvements which had been realized, the main thrust of his message was to reiterate a teaching which had been too little heeded. His could hardly be called a "revolutionary" message (although he, too, was labeled "Communist" by ultraconservatives), but its result was to introduce a new concept into Christian moral teaching. Up to that time it had been taught that justice was of three kinds: "legal justice," which concerned the obligations of individuals to the society of which they were members; "distributive justice," which looked to the obligations of society (represented by government) to its individual members; and "commutative justice," which defines the obligations of individuals (or groups) to each other. In each of these, of course, to speak of "obligations" is to speak of the "rights" which correspond to them. The new concept which resulted from *Quadragesimo Anno* was that of "social justice," which concerns the rights and obligations of social classes in their relations to each other. It is true that neither Leo XIII nor Pius XI called for the abolition of classes altogether—probably because the only theory which did demand this was unacceptable on other grounds—but they did demand that concrete steps be taken to equalize the rights of different classes; which is, I realize, from a Marxist point of view a contradiction in terms, since it is the opposition growing out of inequality which constitutes classes as classes. In any event, this was a step in the right direction.

Quite frankly, although Pope Pius XII did contribute to the literature on this subject, I do not find that there is substantively anything new in his contribution. To a certain extent the same might be said of John XXIII's *Mater et Magistra*, although the emphasis he gives to developing social structures does, it seems to me, provide a foundation for a novel interpretation of social relationships and for a more concrete implementation of social reforms. With *Pacem in Terris*, on the other hand, I believe that

John XXIII did strike out in a new and significant direction. Apart from concrete proposals for securing peaceful relations among peoples throughout the entire world he makes it quite clear that he regards effective aid for social and economic development of the less-developed areas of the world as a major requirement of our day. Inseparable from this is the demand that measures be taken to remedy the unequal situation of the disadvantaged, whether they be peoples or classes of people.

All that I have said so far leads to the need of a more detailed consideration of what may well become *the* classic of Catholic social teaching in the future which opens up before us. I refer to the encyclical *Populorum Progressio* of Pope Paul VI, which, as its title indicates, is oriented toward a solution of the most complex and perplexing problems of our day, the development of man's (all men's) potentialities throughout the entire world on all levels—economic, social, political, cultural. Most significant in this is the recognition that development is meaningless if it is not self-development, which can take place only if men—and the societies to which they belong—are autonomous, independent. Before going into this, however, it might be well for me to pause and listen to your reactions to the development up to this point.

Garaudy:

Historically, traditional Christianity has frequently made the nonbeliever feel that faith implies a retreat from the world, a turning in on self or into the sanctuary.

Is it true that there is in life a special time, a special place, or a special activity called "cult," which is particularly significant for responding to one's interpretation of God?

Does not the death of Christ, a scandal for all previous religions, signify on the contrary a total solidarity with the world, excluding the possibility of fencing off a particular domain of the sacred, of enclosing a religious segment of life?

Now, if the word of God cannot be circumscribed in the formulas of a catechism or even of a creed, if the word of God is an activity, in the very sense in which Jesus is the Word of God, in what human actions, what historical events, be they political or social, is the Church to read the gestures of God?

Does not this essential reading of the "signs of the times," to use the expression of Pope John, consist in searching humbly, i.e. with nothing but the resources of a totally human intelligence—without claiming to transcend history with its gropings, its errors, its failures— for the organization of human relationships which most fully guarantees to each man the possibility of so utilizing his capacities and talents as to be a creator?

Is not that the profoundest content of human hope, not beyond life or history, but in this fleshly life with its history, wherein takes place the most moving dialogue of the human and the divine?

Is it not, then, the task of the Church to be at the side of all those—be they believers or unbelievers, heretics or atheists—who make this hope visible on the horizon of man?

The concrete realization of this task demands infinitely more than individual beneficence or ecclesiastical charity; it demands a basic redistribution of wealth and power.

That, fundamentally, brings into question what is customarily called "the social teaching of the Church."

It would be putting it mildly to repeat the remark of Jaurès, that the Church has begun to concern itself with the weak only when they have become a force. Thus, *Rerum Novarum*, the first "social encyclical," appeared forty-three years after the *Communist Manifesto* and twenty-seven years after the First International. More significantly, it followed the *Syllabus* and, to speak more generally, came after the anathema launched a century before against all political and social revolutions.

There is no point here, however, in uncovering past controversies. More fruitful is a look toward the rising sun. In so doing we must take pains to define with clarity the next step to be taken in order to bridge the chasm which has opened up between the Church and those who love the future.

On the level of social reality the essential obstacle is the fact that when the "Church's social teaching" is defined in relation to capitalism and socialism, it is based on a tragic postulate, according to which: "The right of individual property is not derived from human laws but from nature; public authority, therefore, cannot abolish it" (*Rerum Novarum*). *Quadragesimo Anno* adds, "It is from nature and, *therefore, from the Creator* that men have received the right of private property." In his turn Pius XII reminds us that private property is "the guarantee of the human person's essential freedom."

The encyclical *Mater et Magistra*, referring to *Rerum Novarum*, emphasizes that "private property, including that of productive goods, even of the means of production . . . is a natural right which the State may by no means suppress."

The practical conclusion of such an attitude was drawn with utmost clarity in *Rerum Novarum:* "Let it, then, remain as well established that the proper foundation to be laid down by all those who sincerely desire the good of the people is the inviolability of private property. . . . The socialist theory of collective ownership is . . . contrary to the natural rights of individuals."

On the basis of this principle the Church has unceasingly condemned socialism in its very essence, whereas she condemns only the abuses of capitalism.

The question is whether this "principle" is theological or whether it merely expresses the survival of a Constantinian political tradition whose constant aim has been to give a theological foundation, first to slavery, then to serfdom, before giving its sanction to the system of capitalist private property and to its corollary, the wage contract.

It is not for me to give a theological answer to this question but only to recall that, historically speaking, private ownership of the means of production has led capitalism to the worst forms of oppressing and crushing the individual—in the European proletariat as well as in the colonies. For, just as it is true that private ownership, particularly of the means of production, equips the individual to promote his own aggrandisement, so too, it surrenders, unarmed, to this aggrandisement all those who do not enjoy this private ownership of the means of production. Capitalism, then, is in principle destructive of the freedom about which it boasts.

An elementary logic, which in a century and a half of capitalist expansion has been provided with the most bloody of historical verifications, demonstrates that, if ownership is the guarantee of freedom, then collective ownership of the large means of production is required if the freedom of every man (and not merely of the privileged) is to be guaranteed, if the freedom of the enormous propertyless majority is not to be sacrificed in favor of a privileged handful who, through the ownership of the means of production, absolutely dominate their fellow men. This collective ownership must be established in order that all men may exercise initiative and responsibility in economic matters, in the production and distribution of the goods which condition the development of each and all.

So true is this that one of the next steps to take—thus meeting the expectations of large masses (of believers as well as unbelievers)—is to reverse "the Church's social teaching." This means that, in the light of long historical experience and in the spirit of our times, the Church, instead of condemning socialism in principle and merely the excesses of capitalism, would condemn capitalism in principle and only the perversions of socialism.

Undoubtedly, the encyclical *Populorum Progressio* signals a beginning of change: Its formulations are more nuanced. It subordinates all rights, including those of property and free trade, to the primary human exigency of "promoting the growth of all men and of the whole man." It declares, therefore, that "private property is not for anyone an unconditional and absolute right."

Nevertheless, its practical conclusions remain timid: It condemns "a certain capitalism" and not the very principle of the system.

Some have been too quick to find a revolutionary content in the formula, "The common good, then, sometimes demands expropriation." But expropriation for reasons of public utility has nothing to do with socialism as it is practiced by even the most conservative of socialist governments.

On the other hand, revolution is condemned, "except in the case of evident and prolonged tyranny." This means that it is "a certain capitalism," or "the fundamental principle of liberalism regulating commercial transactions which is here questioned." In no sense is it the very principle of capitalism. It seems that some sort of state capitalism is considered acceptable; in any event, the principle of collective ownership of the means of production is not invoked, nor is the name "socialism" even mentioned. The previous "social" encyclicals, from *Rerum Novarum* on, are not only not repudiated but are rather referred to right in the preamble as having correctly "shed the light of the Gospel on the social questions of their times."

Still, the movement traced out is irreversible. Even if official texts as yet reflect only feebly the metamorphosis taking place, the forward drive of men is being expressed with ever increasing force.

Thus, for example, after the encyclical on development a group of bishops of the "third world," from Latin America, Asia, and Africa, animated by its spirit and enlarging on it, at the generous prompting of the Brazilian Archbishop Helder Camora, has already sketched the doctrinal contours of the Church's proximate future.

Sensitive to the anger of the peoples among whom they live, they are concerned with breaking the bond which links their Church to the colonialist and capitalist system of oppression. They recall St. John's solemn warning in the Apocalypse to the Christians of Rome who oppress the people and traffic in slaves: "Come out of her my people, that you may not be involved in her guilt, nor share the plagues that fall upon her" (18:4).

They assert forcefully that the Church cannot be committed to any one political, social, and economic system: "Once a system ceases to assure the common good, looking only to the interests of a few, the Church should not only denounce the injustice but also separate itself from the evil system, ready to collaborate with another system more just and better adapted to the needs of the time."

If giving up privileges has not been voluntary, "let us at least be able to recognize the hand of God . . . in the events which oblige us to make this sacrifice."

While condemning émigrés from revolutionary countries, who, under religious pretenses, "are in reality fleeing only to save their wealth and privileges," the bishops add, "for a century the Church has tolerated a capitalism . . . scarcely in conformity with the morality of the prophets and of the Gospel. She can only rejoice, how-

ever, to see humanity greet the appearance of another social system, less foreign to this morality."

Citing "true socialism" they declare: "Rather than stand
aloof from it, we should be able to adhere to it joyfully,
as to a form of social life more in accord with the spirit
of the Gospel. In this way we shall prevent some from confusing God and religion with what oppresses the world
of the poor and of the workers, which is to say with feudalism, capitalism, and imperialism."

Putting aside all equivocation, the bishops' text recalls
the declaration made at the Council by Bishop Franic of
Split: "Today workers are becoming more and more conscious that labor constitutes a part of the human person.
. . . Any buying or selling of labor is a sort of slavery.
. . . The evolution of society is progressing in this direction, even in the system which is said to be not so
sensitive as we are in regard to the human person, i.e.
Marxism."

We find in this text by bishops of the third world perhaps the most advanced expression of the aspirations of
those Christians who think that the task of their Church
in a fragmented world is to make hope visible.

VI SOCIAL DOCTRINE

Lauer:

It would be ridiculous for me to attempt either to defend or to explain away the presence in traditional Christianity of the flight-from-the-world tendency. One could, I think, explain much of it as a protest of the powerless—whose only weapon was love—against the all-too-evident evils of a world dedicated to selfishness. But the fact remains that this otherworldliness—call it antiworldliness—has been prolonged beyond its period of usefulness and has even in some cases turned into a kind of acquiescence in the domination of the world and of man by alien forces.

I should hesitate to say, however, that one remedies this by questioning the validity of choosing special times, places, or ways in which to manifest devotion to God—provided, of course, that we do not make of this a substitute for sharing in God's activity, be it that of self-creation or of creating the conditions which make man's life in this world worthy of God's image. To speak only of my own experience, I have never found that commitment to God—or to Christ and the love He preached—ever stood in the way of a commitment to those whom Christ loved, i.e. all men. It may well be that this commitment to man has not been as effective as it might have been; but all that means is that my commitment to God has not been all that it should be.

What I do not see is that we are searching more humbly for the proper organization of human relationships if we rely only on those human resources which we rather arbitrarily assert are in no way derived. Of course it is the task of the Church to be at the side of all who seek what we should be seeking—whether or not they believe what we believe. I can even admit that many who, in fact, oppose Christianity are seeking it more sincerely than many others who claim to be Christian and are not. It is not, however, the task of the Church—or of Christianity— to seek to promote the advancement of man by denying what man truly is, by denying his true dignity for the sake of securing an autonomy whose affirmation is not humble but proud.

As you already know, I experience no hesitation in agreeing that it cannot—must not—be the Church's primary concern to defend its own privileges or even to guarantee that its own existence will remain unchanged (although it cannot disregard its Founder's promise that it will continue to exist). The Church exists for the sake of men—all men, not merely those who are its members. You are quite right, then, in saying that the Church belongs on the side of all those who want to make real man's hope of being able to put to use his capacities and creative gifts, whether they be believers or unbelievers, heretics or atheists. Personally, I must admit that I myself frequently feel closer to your unbelievers, heretics, and atheists than I do to some of my reactionary "brethren." By the same token, I am not out of sympathy with much that you say in criticism of the Church's "social teaching," although I do not always find the perspective from which you criticize unbiased.

With regard to the teaching of the encyclicals regarding the "right of private property," that is a doctrine which dies hard, and I think it is understandable that it should. Apart from the fact that it makes no distinction between private ownership of the means of production and the ownership of that which is inseparable from individual and family living, it is premised on a structure of society which has not evolved to the point where private property can be called a contradiction. Neither Christianity nor the Catholic Church is alone in looking upon private property as a demand of reason. It is a tradition of the West which finds eloquent defense in the moral writings of Kant and Hegel. That Marx should have seen other possibilities for the future was due, I think, far less to the validity of his rational argumentation than to a kind of prophetic vision of history. What even Christian moralists are beginning to see, however, is that even "natural rights" are a function of the concrete structure of human relations and that, therefore, it is possibile to think that what once was a right can cease to be one—when it fails to express the reality of that structure.

Here, then, it is important to be historical in your criticism. Is it really true "that private ownership of the means of production has led capitalism to the worst forms of oppressing and crushing the individual, among the European proletariat as well as in the colonies"? Or, is it capitalist abuse of this ownership which has so altered the structure of human relations that its form of private ownership is no longer viable? The distinction may be a subtle one, but it does explain the possibility of sincere hesitation to accept the solution you propose.

On the basis of this solution you have criticized even *Populorum Progressio* because its "practical conclusions" are "timid." Only if your theory has been shown to be unquestionably true is that correct. I am inclined to move in the direction of thinking that capitalism as we know it is no longer a valid structure of society, but that does not permit me to think that your solution is the only solution, nor should it permit you to speak of the Pope's failure to condemn capitalism outright as though it were a moral fault on his part. At any rate, let us look at some of the things the encyclical does say and see if we can discern there the beginnings of a social teaching for the future.

One of the things that first strikes me in the encyclical is that it has something to say to practically every one of the points we have touched upon in our discussions. It is, for example, the first papal document I know of which puts great emphasis on the necessity of supplying man's material needs, whether they be those of an individual or of a whole people. It is concerned for those who seek to escape hunger, misery, endemic diseases, and ignorance(1)[1]; it applauds man's seeking "to do more, know more, and have more in order to be more"(6); it insists that, although the Church's mission is spiritual, it must be concerned with man's material progress(13); it subordinates all other rights to man's right to develop and benefit by the material goods of the world(22).

At the same time it recognizes that improving the material situation of man should be oriented to securing for him equality in freedom and human dignity. "It is not just a matter of eliminating hunger nor even of reducing poverty. The struggle against destitution, though urgent and necessary, is not enough. It is a question, rather, of building a world where every man, no matter what his race, religion, or nationality, can live a fully human life, freed from servitude imposed on him by other men or by natural forces over which he has not sufficient control; a world where freedom is not an empty word and where the poor man Lazarus can sit down at the same table with the rich man"(47). This means that "every program, made to increase production, has, in the last analysis, no other *raison d'être* than the service of man"(34); it means that increased literacy is essential to human progress(35); it means, ultimately, that economic development must serve integral development(14).

The encyclical does not hesitate to characterize its own teaching as a "humanism," according to which each man is the principal agent of his own self-fulfillment(15). What it calls for, it is true, is a "transcendent humanism"(16), a "new humanism . . . embracing the higher values of love and friendship, of prayer and contemplation"(20), but it recognizes that a prime humanizing force is work, provided that it is intelligent and free(27). It insists that a humanism isolated from God is an inhuman humanism(42), but it sees the elimination of intolerable material conditions as essential to human dignity(9).

Although it can scarcely be said that Pope Paul is endorsing Marxist socialism—he sees it as a doctrine "which respects neither the religious orientation of life to its final end nor human freedom and dignity"(39)—he does insist that it is wrong that profit should be the key motive of economic progress or that competition be the supreme law of economics; he states, in fact, that private ownership of the means of production is not an absolute right(26), that no one group should make progress at the expense of another(44), that private property must never be allowed to conflict with public need(23). He even recognizes that revolution can be necessary, although it almost inevitably produces new kinds of injustice; and he warns that "real evil should not be fought against at the cost of greater misery"(31).

Perhaps one of the most significant contentions which the Pope makes is that "sharing with those in need is an obligation which justice and not merely charity imposes"(23). That this is not to be understood merely on the small scale is evidenced by the claim that man cannot develop unless all humanity develops in a spirit of solidarity(43), that wealthy *nations* have an obligation to help poor ones(49), that the sort of political pressure or economic suzerainty which is so frequently connected with giving be eliminated(52), and that a world fund be set up from just part of the money spent on arms, a fund to be distributed without political or economic strings attached(51).

All in all, the document is epoch-making. It would be unrealistic to expect everyone to be satisfied with every element in it, just as it would be unrealistic to expect that the weight of the Pope's authority can assure the implementation of its provisions in the immediate future. By the same token, it would be naïve to think that it has said all that need be said, that there does not remain room for a lot more saying and a lot more doing. The fact remains that it has been written, and the only direction in which we can move from it is forward.

Garaudy:

On the whole, I am in agreement with the main points of your analysis. I should like, however, to draw your attention to two facts which bring out a certain discordance between words and actions. At the very time when Pope Paul VI was condemning, in terms which are sometimes excellent, both colonialism and neocolonialism, and when he pointed up with generosity the problem of underdevelopment, these problems had become particularly acute in two parts of the world: in Vietnam and in Angola, where Portugal, as the last country in the world to uphold openly the colonial principle, is waging a bloody war against the Angolese people struggling for liberation. Now, with regard to precisely these two situations an energetic stand on the part of the Pope could have played a decisive role. Yet, not only does the encyclical not even allude to them, but no official word or action of the Pope has publicly disavowed Cardinal Spellman's attempt to present the war in Vietnam as a "holy war." As for Portugal, where the Church plays an important official role, where an intervention by the Pope would have had a profound influence, and where that influence could have put an end to the war in Angola and to the colonialist scandal, he instead visited Fatima, to the great joy of the fascist dictator Salazar—nor while there did he say a word about the war in Angola.

There is question then of something much more serious than "doctrinal timidity": It is not true that you are defending the oppressed if you do not condemn their oppressors and oppose them with vigor.

If the encyclical *Populorum Progressio* does not provide the necessary condemnation of this oppression, here is the way we Marxists concretely analyze it.

A true independence, a true democracy, is a regime which gives to each child, to each man, all the means to develop fully all the human riches which are present in each.

To take but the most familiar example, look at Latin America, where the wealthiest and most powerful nation in the Western Hemisphere intervenes with economic and military aid. The over-all population of these nominally independent nations, whose soil is endowed with fabulous riches, numbers 200 millions, of whom 140 million human beings are undernourished and 100 million are illiterate.

On a visit to my country in July 1965, Eduardo Frei, the Christian Democrat President of Chile, declared quite honestly: "The problem of Latin America is not one of petroleum, sugar, or any raw material whatever; it is the problem of man." Acutely conscious that there cannot be a free man in an enslaved nation, President Frei added: "The United States is a great world-power whose hegemony extends to many parts of the world. We cannot challenge so great a power, but among the peoples of Latin America there exists a profound aspiration to a veritable political and economic independence."

The whole historical evolution of the past twenty years, with the irreversible movement toward national liberation among peoples who have long been colonialized, attests the universality of this aspiration.

As the peoples of Asia and Africa begin to develop they reveal the major tendency of this century—a new sharing of historical initiative. Peoples long looked upon as *objects* to be *manipulated* at will want to become active subjects of history. Slaves are becoming men; that is the new sense of life. That is what explains the universal rejection of colonialism.

There are, however, certain methods of economic and military aid—or intervention—which perpetuate the colonial system.

The colonial system was in principle a form of international division of labor which was developed in the eighteenth and nineteenth centuries for the exclusive profit of industrial countries.

What defines the colonial situation essentially is the reduction of some countries to the role of an agricultural or mining appendage to an industrial homeland and the using of these countries as markets for the export of manufactured products and especially of capital from the homeland. Political and military domination was only a *means* to the attainment of this end.

The resulting situation is such that formal recognition of a country's political independence in no way excludes that, for example, through economic aid a country can be kept in colonial subjection, with all the material and human alienations which that involves. Neocolonialism arises from the continuance of unequal exchange between capitalist states and those states which were formerly colonies.

I say "capitalist states" advisedly, for the perpetuation of underdevelopment and of economic and political dependence follows necessarily from the system of direct investment on the part of capitalistic monopolies.

It is easy to derive the objective law of such investments. In countries where they place their investments monopolies do not develop industries which could create the conditions for economic independence, but only branches which will yield the most immediate profits.

The first obvious consequence of investments such as these is the deformation of the economy in countries where they are made. Most often this deformation consists in exclusive emphasis on agricultural products or raw materials. Of Brazilian exports coffee constitutes 74 percent; in Bolivia, tin 60 percent; in Costa Rica, bananas 60 percent; in Chile, copper 63 percent; Santo Domingo, sugar 60 percent; Venezuela, petroleum 95 percent.

Venezuela exports in the raw state its "iron mountain" of Ciudad Bolivar to the steel mills of the United States. In Africa, to avoid the risk of nationalization, foreign capitalist enterprises have chosen to process alumina in Guinea and aluminum in Cameroon.

Thus is perpetuated the colonial system's old "trade economy," an elementary circuit which keeps the market of finished products in the home country and condemns the colony to produce only raw materials without processing them at the source. As M. Dumont, a specialist, writes: "We find, after a lapse of several centuries, in almost the same form, the schema of the former India Company."

In his *Esquisse d'une théorie de l'économie dominante*, François Perroux emphasizes that one-product economies are an essential factor in economic and political dependence. What could be more evident? The system of capitalist investment imposes on the countries of Latin America an economic structure such that the very life of these countries depends on exporting certain products, thus putting them at the mercy of buyers. When, in 1932, Cuba made a somewhat timid effort to secure independence, the United States, which imported five million bags of Cuban sugar annually, reduced the number to two million for the following year. It was give in or die.

The master of the market, i.e. the United States, imposes minimum prices. Thus, in 1958 Brazil exported millions of bags of coffee more than in 1948; but it received for them a million dollars less.

The formula, "trade not aid," remains an hypocrisy so long as the rates for raw materials are not stabilized, which is to say, so long as the buying power of poor countries is not protected.

The most immediate result of this permanent commercial imbalance for countries who are victims of unequal exchanges is a constant increase of their foreign debt. For fourteen countries in Latin America their foreign debt has gone from $1,741,000,000 in 1950 to $5,535,000,000 in 1961; it has tripled in ten years!

In these circumstances aid becomes humiliating, and so-called "gifts" aggravate the consequences of investments. This is true for two reasons. First of all, from the economic point of view, gifts, like investments, are a function not of the needs of the people helped but of the need which the giver has to unload surplus. Secondly, from the political point of view, the fear that the gifts will be halted increases the dependence of those aided.

The International Monetary Fund is composed of delegates from different countries. Its administration and the distribution of votes are in proportion to the contribution of each—one vote for every $100,000. Because the United States contributes 70 percent of the total, the structure of the organization and its decisions express, under the aegis of the United Nations, the will of the United States alone. As an example, due to the demands of this organization, Brazil was obliged to double the dollar rate, i.e. to increase by 100 percent the price it paid for equipment and to reduce by a half the value of the raw materials it exports.

The coping stone of this system of unequal exchanges is what is called "the free movement of capital" or "free convertibility," so traditional has it become to give to each form of slavery the name "freedom." It means, in fact, affording financial enterprises the unhindered possibility of bringing back to their own country benefits in the form of revenue, interest, and the amortization of invested capital.

The global result of the operation is that for every dollar invested in Latin America the monopolies bring back two to the United States. From 1955 to 1958, $1,000,000,095 were invested in Brazil, and $2,000,000,020 were exported. From 1950 to 1955 the United States invested $2,000,000 in Mexico and gained $3,500,000 in profits.

Experience proves that the profits realized by foreign monopolies from such investments perpetuate underdevelopment and aggravate economic and political dependence in countries which are nominally independent. *Populorum Progressio* draws attention to this fact.

The example of Brazil is significant. It is a mistake to believe that it is a state which imports capital. In reality, it continues to export dollars to the United States. This comes about through the simple function whereby capital is repatriated. From the fact that periodically inflation (made necessary by a decline in the value of the raw materials exported) compels a readjustment in the price of industrial equipment, the amortization of factories is extremely rapid, and, on the average, at the end of six to eight years the total invested capital has been repatriated.

Thus it was that, in 1961, Brazil sent to the United States $220,000,000 more than it had received. Averell Harriman was correct when he spoke of "aid" to underdeveloped countries: "It is a fund of aid to the United States." This formula can seem cynical—and, in fact, it is—but according to the U.N. report of 1955 it is mathematically exact: From 1946 to 1951 the United States invested $1,600,000,000 in Latin America and brought home $3,000,000,000 as a result.

An additional fact with regard to Latin America is that there have been cases where factories whose initial investment had been several times amortized by a combination of the mechanism of inflation and that of repatriated capital were then paid for once more, when their owners were reimbursed at the time of nationalization, even though the equipment had become outmoded and useless.

For this reason, on July 9, 1965, in an interview for *Correio de Manha,* the Bishop of Saint Andrew of São Paulo, Jorge Marcos, called for an expropriation of foreign enterprises without indemnity. Speaking of the American electrical firm "Bond and Share," he declared that such enterprises "own a material which has been transformed into scrap iron and should not, therefore, be indemnified at the time of their nationalization." He added: "These enterprises have been paid for over and over again. They cannot then be bought by their rightful owners, the Brazilian people."

One of the last characteristics—and not the least—of these American investments, making of them an impediment to development of the "aided" countries, is that they are military.

Almost 80 percent of United States investments in underdeveloped countries are military. They create armies which have to purchase their arms and equipment in the United States. So true is this that from 85 percent to 90 percent of "aid" credits serve to pay for arms ordered from the United States. This permitted the Undersecretary of State to say: "The greater part of this program, then, reverts to the American economy."

The same is true for South Korea, Pakistan, Turkey, and, as we shall see, for South Vietnam.

In order to impose such a policy on the countries where it invests and which it "aids," the United States is forced to rely not on the people but exclusively on parasitic groups: owners of landed estates, military cadres, and political adventurers, whom it binds to itself by a systematic policy of corruption, as the Prime Minister of Singapore, Lee Kuan Yew, revealed on September 1, 1965.

In Africa, for example, the greatest amount of aid was granted to the worst racists of South Africa. The bank of Dillon, Read and Company, which is that of the United States Secretary of the Treasury, is the investment bank for the government of Pretoria. American investments in South Africa went from $86,000,000 in 1943 to $600,000,000 in 1960.

Another important partner in Africa is the last overtly colonial power, Portugal. Thus, for example, the United States refused to construct a railroad between Northern Rhodesia and Tanganyika because of its ties to Portugal; it wanted to make sure that all exports from Northern Rhodesia would pass through Angola.

In Latin America the history of United States investments is a history of the permanent violation of these countries' national sovereignty, of economic and military aggression, of putting in power the most corrupt and most servile dictators.

To guarantee both the security of and the profit on monopolistic investments the United States has imposed on subservient governments the devaluation of national currencies, wage controls, restriction of credit granted to national industries and of public investments, return at a low price to foreign monopolies of enterprises which had been nationalized, and numerous "service contracts" like those which Frondizi had with Standard Oil.

To give but one example, the common declaration of Brazil and the United States in 1955 "demands the inclusion in the antiinflationist program of the Brazilian Government of measures toward a reduction of government expenditures in all areas, a reduction of the Bank of Brazil's credits, as well as a cutback, based on a more realistic price-policy, in financing communal services controlled by the government."

Such flagrant violations of national sovereignty and such serious harm inflicted on all social strata among the people have led the United States to rely only on the most backward and most corrupt elements. From this follows logically a monstrous hypertrophy of police and military apparatus in order to impose on entire peoples a regime which they hate—the Argentine Army devours 50 percent of the national budget.

The most typical, the most actual, and the bloodiest example of the incompatibility between this kind of aid and the independence of peoples is today furnished by Vietnam. All the mechanism of economic, political, and military intervention which I have analyzed up to this point have there played an outstanding role. The results are overwhelming.

From the economic point of view, American "aid" to South Vietnam has led to collapse and chaos. The economy imposed on South Vietnam by American aid manifests all the marks of the old colonial "trade" economy, aggravated by war and corruption. The result is rising prices and inflation, i.e. the misery of the masses.

American investments have not helped industrial development, since essentially they constitute military aid.

As early as the period 1954-58 defense aid represented 99 percent of total aid; "technical cooperation,"
but 1 percent.

No doubt defense aid does not consist uniquely in
military arms and equipment. The major portion of this
aid goes into procuring merchandise for South Vietnam.
An account in dollars is opened in Washington, and this
account is debited as Vietnamese purchases are made,
while their importers pay their own government in
piasters. It is the mechanism of "return funds."

In addition, the list of goods which can be bought is
not drawn up by the South Vietnamese Government but
by the American Administration of International Cooperation (AIC), which is motivated by a desire to liquidate
American surpluses. Thus, an annual import of from 150
to 200 million piasters worth of cigarettes and tobacco
has forced numerous planters of Tay-Minh, Sadec, and
Gia to abandon their crops. Factories have had to release
their personnel. In the textile industry, the country's
principal industry, cotton production has fallen from
2600 to 500 tons since 1957. Of the 12,000 looms in the
country, with a productive capacity of 100 million meters
of cloth, only half are functioning, and production has
fallen to 60 million meters.

The economic situation brought about by American
aid involves in South Vietnam the same consequences as
elsewhere: the anger of the people and the necessity of
relying on the most docile and the most corrupt military
and political adventurers. With governments completely
cut off from the people and remaining in power only
with the help of American military force, this has led to
cascades of *coups d'état*, as in Latin America.

Obviously, then, under these conditions the United
States had to oppose the free elections foreseen for 1956
by the Geneva Convention. President Eisenhower in his
book indicates the reasons for American opposition to

these elections. The reports of our news services, he writes, show that if these elections had taken place, Ho Chi Minh would have had 80 percent of the votes in South Vietnam and an overwhelming majority in North Vietnam.

There as elsewhere, then, the alternative was to rely on a military dictatorship and to count on force alone in opposition to the will of an entire people, to the south as well as to the north of the seventeenth parallel.

In defining the American Administration's policy in Vietnam as one which systematically violates the Vietnamese people's right of self-determination, the Geneva Convention, and the Charter of the United Nations, Senator Wayne Morse said in May 1965, at Reed College, Oregon: "The report of the Senate Foreign Affairs Committee is packed with concordant testimony adding up to one conclusion: between 80 percent and 90 percent of the Vietcong are South and not North Vietnamese; and between 80 percent and 90 percent of the arms captured are American, not from North Vietnam, Russia or China. . . .

"At the present time, for a population of approximately 15 million inhabitants in South Vietnam, the military numbers between 500 and 700 thousand. . . . What figures does the Administration give us on the military strength of the Vietcong? Between 25 and 35 thousand. Now, who at present controls more than 75 percent of the territory of South Vietnam? The Vietcong, and not government forces."

To conclude, it will be sufficient to summarize the lessons revealed by the foregoing analysis.

1. The first criterion for an aid which favors development and creates the economic bases of independence is the following: Does such aid contribute to the development of a country's productive forces; does it promote a

balanced *industrialization?* For that there are a number of necessary conditions.

First of all, we have seen the evil done by direct investments by capitalist enterprises. The congress of Latin American economists, held in Mexico, June 1965, published the following final resolution: "Direct foreign investments produce effects which are unfavorable to the accumulation of capital and to the balance of payments, they have a deleterious influence on foreign trade, and they result in the subordination of national enterprises."

To avoid such harmful consequences it is preferable that the help come not from a private enterprise but from the state. In addition, it should not take the form of an investment but of a loan. The loan should be repayable not in foreign currency but in national products.

The United Nations conference on trade and development, held at Geneva, June 15, 1964, says this in its final resolution: "This assistance should not be subjected to conditions, whether they be political, economic, military, or other."

From this point of view the contrast is striking between the stagnation of South Vietnam and the economic expansion in the North. Soviet aid was given for industrial equipment: machine factory in Hanoi, electric power plant in Uong Bi, modernization of mines in Dong Trieu. Chinese aid created the first ironworks. As a result, between 1955 and 1965 North Vietnam has been able to develop its industry at an average increase of from 15 percent to 20 percent annually.

This aid may take the form of loans or of gifts: It has never taken the form of an investment such that the benefits realized would be for the exclusive profit of the investor country, which would thus be able to realize a normal accumulated income, while paying an interest of only 1 percent to 2 percent. In North Vietnam the accumulation is such that the percentage of the national budget related to aid diminishes steadily—from 38.6 percent in 1955 to 19.8 percent in 1960 (while in South Vietnam it went from 10.8 percent in 1955 to 36.5 percent in 1958). There we have a type of aid which contributes to the creation of economic bases for national independence.

2. Another criterion for an aid which not only respects but favors a national progress toward a veritable independence and individual progress toward a veritable humanity, is the access to education which it affords to all. No doubt "aid," even under the form of crude intervention in the economy and politics of the country aided, does not directly imply the maintenance of illiteracy, since even parasitic enterprises need a work force which will not be illiterate. What it directly hinders is the formation of intermediate or advanced technical forces. Indirectly, however, because it relies on the most backward social forces, this sort of aid results in the continuance of illiteracy.

In Brazil 66 percent of the children do not go to school. In Colombia it is 70 percent, in Bolivia 72 percent, Guatemala 77 percent, Mexico 54 percent, Santo Domingo 55 percent, and in Haiti 80 percent. Whereas in Cuba it is less than 9 percent.

During the last ten years of American domination in Cuba illiteracy did not decrease by 1 percent. In 1961 Cuba counted 979,000 illiterates. In one year of a campaign for literacy the number was reduced by 95 percent; and education was given a decisive impulse on all levels.

How can anyone fail to see that in the whole of a Latin America consigned to misery, slavery, and ignorance by United States intervention, it is Cuba which, thanks to aid from socialist countries, has inaugurated the second war of independence and has thus given shape to the hope of all?

To recapitulate: That aid to a developing country be compatible with and promote its independence its effect must be to develop that country's productive forces by means of a harmonious industrialization, to make possible a genuine agrarian reform, and to make education accessible to all.

For the United States to respect these principles it need renounce nothing. It would on the contrary give back to America the image of great beauty which was traditionally hers. I speak of the Declaration of Independence, which, in the name of human rights, rejected colonial status. I speak of the double principle of noncolonialization and nonintervention proclaimed by Monroe in his 1823 message to Congress. I speak of Lincoln and Roosevelt, of the America which does not inspire in people anger but respect and love.

Lauer:

It behooves me, it would seem, to react in some way to your indictment of Pope Paul for not having condemned the remarks of Cardinal Spellman and the politics of Salazar. Frankly, I should like to have seen him do both, although it might be more humble on both my part and yours to question whether our nice safe indignation as private citizens can be imposed on those who daily live the torture of a responsibility we shall never know. Let us simply admit that the Pope, as well as Cardinal Spellman, can make mistakes—and that we have no idea what our own courage would be, were we in a position where great harm could result, whether we speak or do not speak. On the other hand, let us also recognize that Christian opinion is not monolithically determined and that it has on the whole provided the condemnations you demand.

For the rest, since there is no third party who sets down the rules for our discussion, you are, I suppose, the best judge of what and how much you want to say here. Still, it does seem to me that your lengthy indictment of American international economic policies is somewhat out of proportion in a dialogue between a Marxist and a Christian. It is difficult for me to understand how such an emotion-packed and politically oriented condemnation of what I as a Christian in no way support can significantly contribute to our dialogue. One gets the impression that you really have nothing more to say about Christianity and so you turn to a diatribe against un-Christian capitalism.

Negatively, of course, your description does illustrate what you mean by the national independence you speak of when you say, "Peoples want to become active subjects of history," or, "Slaves are becoming men; that is the sense of history." That comes through in your analysis, but it does seem to me that you are wasting your time going off on a long digression which would be significant only if you could connect it with Christianity. For my part, I simply see no point in disagreeing with you, unless it be to question this or that naïve "statement of fact," interpretation, or insinuation of causal relationship and motivation—none of which would greatly change the grim character of the over-all picture. It might not, however, be amiss to point out that anticapitalist statistics really prove nothing positive with regard to Communism.

With regard to those statistics, I leave it to those who have both more interest and more competence to take you up on those. I do hope, in fact, that someone will take the trouble to examine the accuracy of your statistics and the rationality of your interpretations. With reference to our own discussion, however, I simply did not need this lesson in statistics—accurate or inaccurate —to make me agree with the three points of your solution to the situation. But I cannot escape the impression that there is a certain cynicism operative here, when you make it impossible for a "capitalist" nation to violate the "necessary laws" of its own form of production by giving aid altruistically, with no ulterior motives, but fail to see the other "necessary law" operative in the one-sided interpretation you give to all "facts." Your "law" seems to demand that *gifts* from capitalist countries must increase dependence, whereas gifts from Communist countries promote independence. The point is that I am no nearer to being convinced now than I was before that your process of constructing "laws" is a valid one.

Nevertheless, I see no reason to dispute either your figures or your interpretations; even if they are incorrect, the fact of economic dependence is there, it is evil, and I am convinced that it should be changed. Actually, I did not need all this in order to be persuaded that only under some form of socialism can a solution be found at all. But I still need a lot of convincing that Communism is the form demanded. Your suggestion, for example, that underdeveloped countries would be helped more by loans than by investments may well be a good one, but if the price to be paid for this is the sort of government ownership of capital which Communism advocates, I am not sure that the cure might not be as bad as the illness.

All this brings me back to a question that I hinted at earlier. If I read you correctly, you have been contending all along that the only solution to the ills which face us is Marxist (Communist) socialism. The question is whether that is even a genuinely dialectical solution. If Christianity and Communism can really dialogue, and not merely discuss—or debate—there would seem to have to be a sense in which they are dialectically related to each other. This means not merely opposition but mutual determination. We have seen development on each side; if nothing more, each has progressed in the awareness of its own implications. What I am looking for here—in fact, what I see—is something more. Their dialectical relationship to each other influences the development of each. Here, of course, I can speak with assurance of Christianity, which, in a century of confronting Marxism, has become gradually more aware of its own social implications. I should like to think, however, that in a century of confronting Christianity—more significantly in recent years, when dialogue has become a "real possibility"— Marxism has developed by integrating much that Christianity has to offer. This sort of mutual integration *can*, of course, be by way of simply borrowing, but in terms of dialectical development it should be more than that.

Now, if it is essential to development that what develops also remains what it has been all along, the progress of the two sides of such a relationship would consist in their becoming more like each other while remaining what they are. I can see this happening in Christianity—witness the increased emphasis on its "humanist" character. I should like to think that the same is true of Marxism. If it is, then I ask whether it is not possible that Marxist socialism might continue to be what it is and yet cease to be "Communist" socialism, not only from the point of view of the outsider, who may well see it erroneously, but also from that of the insider who, presumably, refuses to predict what forms it can and cannot take. Previously I asked whether you foresaw the possibility of complete religious liberty within a Marxist society. You responded affirmatively, but your answer did not say whether this would ultimately mean a change in Marxist society itself. What I am asking now is whether you can foresee the possibility of a Marxist society which would not be a "Communist" society. Nor need such a question necessarily imply a negative judgment regarding Communist society; what it is asking is whether the Communist form—in any or all of its manifestations in our contemporary world—

could turn out to be a stage to be superseded in the developmental process.

It would, of course, be expecting too much were I to ask you to fill in the details of what such a change might imply. It would, nevertheless, go a long way toward allaying mistrust if we could foresee that the resolution of contradictions must not necessarily come to a dead end in ultimate unresolvable contradiction. As I mentioned before, I am prepared to recognize the substantive validity of your indictment of the way in which "capitalist" practice has *de facto* resulted in the exploitation, impoverishment, and enslavement of hundreds of millions in all its spheres of influence. Only if we are both sincerely concerned to put an end to this sort of thing in the name of man can we be said to agree at all. My problem is the price to be paid for putting an end to it. At present I feel that the price is too high, if it means the permanence of Communism as it manifests itself today.

Garaudy:

Some theoretical definitions will not be out of place, if the question is to be made more precise. As you know, even in the tradition of the utopian socialists, like Fourier or Saint-Simon, socialism is a transitional stage in the passage from capitalism to Communism.

The characteristics of socialism in contrast to capitalism are the following:

1) From the economic point of view: collective rather than private ownership of the means of production.

2) From the political point of view: hegemony of the working class substituted for the hegemony of the bourgeoisie (i.e. owners of the means of production).

3) From the cultural point of view: the accessibility for each child, no matter what his social origin, of the highest form of culture, and a transformation of this cul-

ture itself such that it will no longer be inspired by individualism and competition but by a community spirit, according to which the freedom of my neighbor is not the limit of my freedom but rather its condition.

Communism is distinguished from socialism, which is but a preparation, a first stage.

1) From the economic point of view: by the fact that "penury," which has reigned since the origins of humanity, is overcome thanks to technical progress. It is no longer necessary, therefore, to distribute goods according to the socialist formula, "to each according to his work"; rather the Communist formula is, "to each according to his needs." Such a distribution of material goods is in our age a possible, an accessible horizon, if we cease to waste on armaments an enormous part of our production.

2) From the political point of view: Communism implies the disappearance of the state. The state is an instrument for defending the interests of one class. When classes disappear and with them the domination of one class over another, the existence of the state has no object. There is no call for some men to repress others but only for all to manage in common their common wealth. According to Saint-Simon's formula, which Marx adopted, "To the government of men will succeed the administration of things." The disappearance of class antagonisms and the universal accessibility of culture will permit man to arrive at a situation where, since every citizen feels himself responsible to all, each one will think and act as a statesman.

3) From the cultural point of view: Communism is the realization of *integral man,* i.e. man no longer mutilated by the division of labor and by specialization. Communism implies *the disappearance of the separation between intellectual and manual labor.*

Thus, if we stick to *theoretical* definitions, socialism, which is only a transitional stage, is inconceivable without Communism, which is nothing else but the full realization of the former.

I believe, however, that your question can have two other senses: (1) Can socialism be instituted by other parties than the (Marxist) Communist party? (2) Or, are the models realized up to now by Communist parties the only possible models?

With regard to the first point, it in no way follows from the principles of Marxism that in a socialist regime power should be exercised by one party alone, the Communist party. If this latter did obtain in the Soviet Union, that was in no way due to reasons of principle but rather for historical reasons. In April 1917, Lenin considered it desirable that there be a coalition government, including various socialist parties. Only when the bourgeois and then the socialist parties turned to the side of armed counterrevolution and when they relied on a foreign invasion against their own country did they exclude themselves from power. Even thereafter Lenin always insisted that this situation was consequent upon historical conditions and the international setup. A more proximate example is that of Bulgaria, where power is exercised conjointly by the Communist party and the Peasant party, an ancient traditional party with deep roots in the peasantry, which had had a profound influence on the orientation of Bulgarian politics. Its participation has made it possible to solve agricultural problems better than in certain other socialist countries where the Communist party alone is in power.

In a country like France, with its ancient parliamentary traditions (which existed neither in Russia nor in China) and with its strongly structured and organized political parties, it is highly probable that the parliament and the various parties will play an important role in the construction of socialism. Waldeck Rochet, Secretary General of the Communist party in France, has more than once developed the thesis that in France it is not only probable but also desirable that socialism be constructed with the cooperation of a *number* of parties. He has even made it clear that parties in opposition to socialism will not be deprived of their means of expression and that all that will be demanded of them will be to accept democratically the law of the majority.

All this means that several *models* of socialism are possible in accord with the historical traditions proper to each people and with the previous social structure. It is obvious, for example, that the model of socialism will be different when there is question of a country passing directly from a feudal regime to socialism (as in China), of one which passes from a backward capitalism to socialism (as in Russia), or of one which goes directly from a developed form of capitalism—monopolistic state capitalism—to socialism (as will be the case in France).

Lauer:

Your answer (or answers) to my last question rather surprises me. One has grown accustomed to look upon Communists as hard-headed planners for a discernible future—even to admire the consistency of their planning—and here you turn out to be as utopian as the most "utopian socialist." I realize, of course, that to speak in terms of theoretical definitions is to speak in an ideal way without predicting that the ideal will be realized totally as it has been conceived. Still, your optimism is such that you actually foresee not only an end to all present class antagonisms but also the nonintrusions of other forms of class antagonism in a Communistic society. Hypothetically, of course, this would have to be true, since one could quite well say that, if such class antagonisms do arise, Communistic society had not yet in truth arrived.

Thus, I have no difficulty in agreeing that it *would* be nice if society could develop to a stable situation in which it would be permanently true that the distribution of material goods would leave absolutely no one's need unsatisfied (it would also have to guarantee that no one's desires would exceed his needs). I suspect that no one would deny that this is an attractive ideal, but I feel sure there will continue to be considerable skepticism on two points: (1) that such a paradise really does await us here on earth; and (2) more significantly, considerable doubt that the course being pursued by Marxist socialism actually will produce this paradise. In fact, the whole thrust of my question is right there: I have seen nothing in Marxist theory or practice that I can construe as evidence that, if all opposition to it vanishes, it will in fact result in the utopia you describe—especially if it does not receive a strong infusion of the kind of faith, hope and love which you call "alienation."

As for the disappearance of the state, that, it would seem, depends on the acceptance of your definition of the state as "an instrument for defending the interests of one class." That, however, I should scarcely call a definition; it is a description of what you think all states up to this time have actually been. If all you mean is that in the ideal order the state should cease to be what it has been, I have no quarrel with you. If you mean that a world society is actually on the way, in which all citizens will be statesmen and that Marxism is ushering it in, I am as skeptical as I was before. If you mean that an ideal society in which all citizens are statesmen will be one with no need of organization and, therefore, of government (however different from past or present governments), I think you are denaturing society.

Finally, with regard to the universality and equality of cultural and educational opportunities, I sincerely hope that the day will come when that is much more than an ideal. I am sure, however, that not even a Marxist thinks that the sort of practice he advocates will produce equality of *talent*. I am not even sure that one can say theoretically that it would be *desirable* to do so. In any event, it would be more realistic not to count on it or to think that "self-creativity" can have that as its goal.

Still, out of all this comes something which one simply cannot fail to admire. Not only is the ideal admirable, but dedication to the ideal is even more so. Even though I cannot share your conviction that you have found the eventual solution to all of men's ills, I cannot but respect the Marxist spirit of sacrifice, the ability of Marxists to work for a future which they as individuals will not share. There is something very noble in the willingness to forego a superficial present satisfaction of their needs for the sake of a future society where needs will be genuine and their satisfaction real. Although it might seem to be stretching a point, I see here another point of similarity between Marxism at its best and Christianity at its best; we cannot share a concern for the future of man and of society without sharing a readiness to make sacrifices, even the supreme sacrifice of dying that others may live—better. Christian teaching has often been misinterpreted as calling for sacrifice either for its own sake or because God is pleased by it. As a matter of fact, Christianity sees sacrifice as worthwhile precisely because it is the price we are willing to pay for the acquisition of something else worthwhile. The negative element of sacrifice derives its value from the positive result to which it looks.

Strangely enough, to speak of future society in this way brings up a topic which neither of us can avoid, the death of the individual, for whom "future society" is inevitably an ideal, never a reality. For me there is something particularly poignant in your speaking of "the alienated notions of transcendence and death"[2] espe-

cially as you obviously did not intend the statement in the
sense in which it comes across to me. I have already discussed the ambiguity of calling transcendence an "alienation," but I feel that saying the same of death makes
admirable sense, a sense, however, which you can scarcely
want to give it—quite the reverse. A death which is final,
"the final limitation,"[3] a death which for the individual
who dies is total, is the worst form of alienation I can
conceive—as Plato saw it, it is the worst possible slur to
the dignity of man. I realize, of course, that you see this
alienation overcome in the immortality of the species:
"By its conquests the species can dream of a real immortality."[4] But I do not see how this disalienates man's personal dignity.

There is unquestionably something very noble in your
refusing (as did Albert Camus) to let hope in an afterlife compromise the grandeur of this one, but it is somewhat beside the point to see in this refusal a triumph of
rationality. Hope in personal immortality does not pretend to be rational, but hope in the "real immortality"
of the species should not pretend to be so either—unless
arguing from "exigency" to "absence" is more rational
than arguing from "exigency" to "presence." In effect,
however, we are not concretely so far apart in our "argumentation." We, you say, pass "from the exigency of
mediation . . . to the presence of a mediator"[5]—which is
not quite true—but, in fact, you do much the same; your
mediator is the "real species" man. We are both convinced that, without a mediator, individual man is lost.
You *believe* that the species satisfies this need; we *believe* that it does not, that it is the mediator who is both
God and man who renders the species capable of satisfy-
ing its need. Now, it is not clear to me why recognizing
man's dignity in this latter way is an "alienation,"[6]
whereas recognizing it in the former way is not. Perhaps
the error is to say that either one of us "argues" from

exigency to presence; it is not from exigency that Christians argue to presence; it is from a positive manifestation of that presence—but that is not arguing, it is *faith*.

Thus, we should both admit what is of faith in our position: I *believe* that the individual person will live after death (which is quite distinct from a neo-Platonic immortality of the soul); you *believe* that not the individual but only the species will go on living (forever) —both of us in the name of the dignity of man. For neither of us is it a matter of "scientific knowledge," nor does either conviction make him who holds it any less committed to the community of men—here and now. We both believe in the solidarity of men—all men—and I do not see how your belief emphasizes that more than mine does. To deprive man of his faith, then, is truly "to strip him of one of his dimensions."[7] If, on the other hand, what Marxist atheism does is to "deprive man only of the illusion of certainty,"[8] we have no quarrel. It is precisely the glory of faith—which, you say so well, is "a particular way of *standing up* before the world"[9]—that it is never rational certainty, always risk. Does Marxist atheism want to deprive man of this risk? Does it think that it is benefiting man in so doing? I am willing to accept that doubt is an "integral part of living faith"[10]; must not the Marxist, too, accept it as an integral part of his living faith?

It is true, then, that in a very real way Marxism can help Christian faith, not by eliminating it—dialogue cannot have that end—but by helping to purge it of its opiate character (I am not about to deny that it can be and sometimes is infected with this character). If Marxism does this it will help Christian faith to be more authentically human and, therefore, more authentically Christian, more authentically religious. In this connection I am sure that authentic Christianity can go along with your de-emphasis on the miraculous and, above all, on the "gross types of apologetic employed"[11] in trying to make science itself an argument for religion—though I must confess that I do not find this "in the majority of religious publications."[12] You must read more "religious publications" than I do—in fact, a publication where I do find this sort of apologetic I do not call "religious."

Garaudy:

With regard to the problem of death, I believe that it is a double one: depending on whether it is a question of one's own death or of another's. In either case, for a Marxist death cannot be considered only as a limit or a negation; it is perhaps one of the elements which reveals the most profound sense of life. Marx defines death as a terrible revenge which the species takes on the individual.

Concerning one's own death, it recalls constantly to each of us that the human project is not an individual project; I cannot limit myself to perspectives which would be mine alone. I am a sort of worker responsible for a project which transcends me. "The terrible revenge which the species takes on the individual," as Marx said, has, then, a sort of pedagogical significance: It forbids limiting the human horizon to that of individualism and egoism. Such is the sense we can give to death, when there is question of our own death.

Then, there is the death of others. There, too, death has not merely the character of scandal, of limit or negation, which is too often spoken of; it has also its pedagogical character. It reminds us of what love is in its highest form: Love is not accomplished in an I-Thou relation alone, but rather in the relation of the I to all. However powerful or deep this love may be, it cannot be exhausted in the relationship between two beings. That is what death recalls to us.

Thus, in both cases death gives life its highest significance. We cannot, then, subordinate life to death, i.e. subordinate life to what would be a reward or a punishment hereafter, nor to what could even be called an immortality of the soul or a resurrection of the body. Death gives to life on earth its full dimension, which is not individual but communal. I do not think that in this we are very far from Biblical tradition or from the highest Christian tradition. I have always been struck, in reading Dante's *Divine Comedy*, by the fact that there is no question of a history of the dead but rather of a judgment on life. For us Marxists, hell, in its medieval form as a place of punishment after this life, has disappeared for the same reason as the pillory or torture among the ancient sanctions which no longer belong to our age. If we have an adult conception of hell, of the afterlife, or of death, that means that we must seek their meaning in this life and not in one which would be its mythical prolongation, whether in punishment or in reward. We Marxists do not imagine eternal life as some form of prolongation before and after our own life, before and after our own history; rather we conceive of it as a certain quality of this life and not of another life. Our life has this dimension of eternity, to the extent that it is not limited to our individuality, to the extent that we are certain of being defined fully as man only in our relationship to the other man, to all men in the totality of their history. Here, once more, I am not sure that we do not find ourselves in agreement with a fundamental teaching of authentic biblical tradition.

To say that, as a result of this necessarily very limited dialogue, we have come to a complete understanding of either our agreements or our disagreements would clearly be to claim too much. What is more, it would be claiming to have accomplished far more than we set out to accomplish. Our aim at the beginning and throughout has been to prepare the ground for a continuing larger dialogue by ceasing merely to talk about dialogue, its possibility, its necessity, its practical conditions, and to let two great conceptions of the world and of man confront each other through the efforts of two of their representatives. We have discovered unsuspected agreements; we have, perhaps, uncovered possibilities of reconciling some disagreements; we have been brought up short before disagreements, the solution of which we can, if at all, only vaguely foresee. Most of all we have learned a great deal; we have been mutually enlightened.

In one sense what we have learned most thoroughly is mutual respect. Not that such a respect was absent before we began; rather it now has a new and more durable foundation, which, paradoxically enough, has been revealed by our disagreements as much as by our agreements. The basic disagreement, we can say, is a philosophical one, but even here the attitudes which oppose each other are both dictated by a fundamentally humanist concern. One of us fears that man is somehow degraded, both theoretically and practically, if his existence and action are conceived of as dependent on God. The other fears that to separate man from God, or from his belief in God, is to make of him an abstraction and that any attempt to concretize him on this basis will but compound the abstraction. Both of us, however, want man to become truly human in a society so structured that it will permit him to develop the initiative, responsibility, and creativity which can be his only if he is genuinely free. Although each may still have doubts as to whether the other's position will really contribute to man's liberation, we are one in our conviction that exploitation, colonialism—whether political or economic—and privilege are not justified in retaining the word "freedom" in their vocabulary.

Here it seems in order to repeat what we said at the beginning, i.e. this has been a dialogue between *a* Christian and *a* Marxist, not a dialogue between Christianity and Marxism. We are convinced, however, that such a limitation neither invalidates the dialogue nor militates against the conviction that the two movements we represent can converge toward a dialectical resolution. This does not involve the claim that we have concretely promoted this resolution, but it does carry with it the hope that in publishing the results of our own meetings we have already contributed to enlarging the dialogue and thus to making resolution a concrete possibility.

It is inevitable, of course, that we shall both be criticized, either because neither has been sufficiently critical of the other or because neither has made a sufficiently strong positive case for his own side. Here it might be well to reiterate that this has not been a capitalist-communist dialogue (since capitalism is not consciously represented at all), nor has it been a dialogue between a Christian and a particular kind of Marxist (although it has been necessary to use particular illustrations which could conceivably engage the very logic of Marxism). Neither of us has any fear of repudiating what either of us considers to be unfaithful either to the essence of what he stands for or to the kind of development its history calls for. It may be that, in choosing to discuss what one considers to be important problems arising under the three headings of religion, morality, and politics, we have left out what one or another reader considers integral to any attempt to dialogue at all. That is really not so bad; it immediately opens up the possiblility of engaging in the continuing dialogue precisely those who are disappointed with this one. In any event, since no arbiter has assigned us a list of topics to be discussed we have felt justified in establishing the rules of the game as we went along. The result has been gratifying to us; we can only hope that it will achieve a larger purpose than our own gratification.

Each of us is aware that he would be more than human were he not to some extent at least the victim of the propaganda to which he is most exposed. This has sometimes made mutual understanding difficult; it has clearly resulted in conflicting interpretations of the same events (which is clearly inevitable, when the lapse of time has not been sufficient to insure historical objectivity). Still, one of the not unimportant results of having dialogued at all has been to dull the effects of propaganda or, at least, to send each one of us back to re-examine the effects which that propaganda has had on him. If it is true to say that two can be more objective than one, it is even truer to say that they will be more objective if the confrontation of their opposing views permits each to re-examine his own in the light of the other's. To begin at all we had to be convinced that not all good will was on one side and all bad will on the other. We have now reached the point of recognizing that there is more good than bad will on both sides. Good will alone, however, is not enough to resolve differences, and this is where mutual enlightenment becomes so important. We believe that the dialogue has meant that for us; we hope that it will contribute toward a similar result for all men of good will.

We make no pretension that we have posed all the problems that could be posed and, even less, that we have resolved all the ones we have posed. What we have done is to engage in discussion on a question which is by no means academic, since on the answer that is given to it depends to a great extent our future.

Both of us, then, hope that a good number of our readers will write to us and thus help us to fill in the gaps and the inadequacies of our common investigation. We hope that our readers will ask questions, suggest new perspectives, present objections, or add depth where our too brief remarks have failed to do so. We should be happy to combine materials such as these with our own replies to our readers' contributions and to publish in another volume a larger dialogue which would comprise such contributions and the reflections which they have occasioned. If this can be done, the dialogue will have ceased to be the affair of two men and will involve all—thus fulfilling the purpose for which this dialogue was instituted in the first place.

NOTES

Introduction:
1. Roger Garaudy, *From Anathema to Dialogue* (trans. Luke O'Neill). New York: Herder and Herder, 1966.
2. Cf. Conference of the World Council of Churches, Geneva, July 1964.

Chapter I:
1. Roger Garaudy, *Marxisme du XXe siècle.* Paris: La Palatine, 1966.

Chapter II:
1. Cf. Karl Marx-Friedrich Engels, *Die heilige Familie.* Berlin: Dietz, 1953, pp. 20, 46, 50–51.
2. *Marxisme du XXe siècle,* p. 173.
3. *From Anathema to Dialogue,* p. 77.
4. *Ibid.,* p. 78.
5. *Ibid.,* pp. 78–79.
6. *Marxisme,* p. 7.
7. *From Anathema,* p. 81.
8. *Ibid.,* p. 86.
9. *Marxisme,* p. 298.
10. Georges Casalis, "Printemps à Marianske Lazne," *Christianisme Social,* 75 (1967), p. 205.
11. *Marxisme,* p. 43.
12. *From Anathema,* p. 46.
13. *Marxisme,* p. 162.
14. *Ibid.,* p. 190.
15. *From Anathema,* p. 49.
16. *Ibid.,* p. 54.
17. *Ibid.,* p. 58.

Chapter III:
1. *XXᵉ Congrès du parti communiste de l'Union Soviétique.* Paris: Cahiers du Communisme, 1956, pp. 441–49.
2. *Ibid.,* pp. 122–23.
3. Cf. *ibid.,* p. 179.
4. *Ibid.,* p. 31.
5. Cf. *ibid.,* pp. 240–41.
6. *Ibid.,* p. 36.
7. *Ibid.,* p. 208.
8. *Ibid.,* p. 252.
9. *Ibid.,* p. 283.
10. *Ibid.,* p. 313.
11. *From Anathema to Dialogue,* p. 71.
12. *Ibid.,* p. 72.
13. *Marxisme du XXᵉ siècle,* p. 58.
14. *Ibid.,* p. 87.
15. *Ibid.,* p. 80.

Chapter IV:
1. *Marxisme du XXᵉ siècle,* p. 32.
2. *Ibid.,* p. 113.
3. *Ibid.,* pp. 97–98.

Chapter V:
1. Harvey Cox, *God's Revolution and Man's Responsibility,* pp. 21–22.
2. Karl Marx-Friedrich Engels, *Communist Manifesto,* Part III.
3. Friedrich Engels, *Ludwig Feuerbach und der Ausgang der klassischen deutschen Philosophie.* Berlin: Dietz, 1951, p. 15.

Chapter VI:
1. The numbers in parentheses refer to the paragraphs of the Encyclical.
2. *From Anathema to Dialogue,* p. 89.
3. *Ibid.*
4. *Marxisme du XXᵉ siècle,* p. 25.
5. *From Anathema,* p. 90.
6. *Marxisme,* p. 164.
7. *From Anathema,* p. 95.
8. *Ibid.,* p. 96.
9. *Ibid.,* p. 115.
10. *Marxisme,* p. 21.
11. *From Anathema,* p. 106.
12. *Ibid.*